# HIGH-IMPACT GOVERNING IN A NUTSHELL

## 17 QUESTIONS THAT BOARD MEMBERS AND CEOs FREQUENTLY ASK

Doug Eadie, President
Doug Eadie & Company

asae | american society of association executives

WASHINGTON, D.C.

Information in this book is accurate as of the time of publication and consistent with standards of good practice in the general management community. As research and practice advance, however, standards may change. For this reason, it is recommended that readers evaluate the applicability of any recommendation in light of particular situations and changing standards.

American Society of Association Executives
1575 I Street, NW
Washington, DC 20005-1103
Phone: (202) 626-2723; (888) 950-2723 outside the metropolitan Washington, DC area
Fax: (202) 408-9633
E-mail: books@asaenet.org
ASAE's core purpose is to advance the value of voluntary associations to society and to support the professionalism of the individuals who lead them.

Susan Robertson, Senior Vice-President, Member Relations and Business Development
Baron Williams, Director, Book Publishing
Arline Williams, Director, Design and Production

Interior design by CimarronDesign.com
Cover design by Debra Moore
Edited by Linda Daily

This book is available at a special discount when ordered in bulk quantities. For information, contact the ASAE Member Service Center at (202) 371-0940.

A complete catalog of titles is available on the ASAE Web site at www.asaenet.org/bookstore

Library of Congress Cataloging-in-Publication Data

Eadie, Douglas C.
    High-impact governing in a nutshell: 17 questions that board members and CEOs frequently ask / Doug Eadie.
        p. cm.
    ISBN 0-88034-250-1
    1. Nonprofit organizations—Management. 2. Corporate governance. 3. Boards of directors. 4. Directors of corporations. 5. Chief executive officers. 6. Leadership. I. American Society of Association Executives. II. Title.
HD62.6.E184 2003
658.4'2—dc22

                                                                    2003063624

Printed in the United States of America.

10 9 8 7 6 5 4 3 2 1

*Dedicated to the Memory of My Father*

*William Clay Eadie*

*A Strong But Gentle Man*

# Table of Contents
## and the 17 Questions

# Foreword

I am delighted that the American Society of Association Executives (ASAE) has published Doug Eadie's *High-Impact Governing in a Nutshell,* continuing ASAE's proud tradition of investing in the advancement of the field of nonprofit leadership and management. Doug's plain-spoken and unpretentious little book is must reading for board members, CEOs, and senior managers of associations and all other members of the large and incredibly diverse family of nonprofit organizations. Based on Doug's hands-on experience in working with hundreds of associations and other nonprofit organizations over the past 25 years, *High-Impact Governing in a Nutshell* is filled with precious nuggets of wisdom that you can put to immediate, practical use in your organization in the interest of strengthening your board's leadership and solidifying the board–CEO partnership.

As you well know, high-impact governing is a preeminent key to organizational success in these challenging times, and the need for practical, tested guidance in developing board leadership capacity has never been greater. Doug's answers to the 17 frequently asked questions that make up this fascinating and insightful look at the board–CEO leadership team are not intended to paint a complete picture of the complex, rapidly changing field of nonprofit governance. However, in my professional opinion as both a CEO and experienced board member, *High-Impact Governing in a Nutshell* arms you with essential information you need in tackling the board-development challenge.

If you are like me, you have probably learned to dread opening a new book on governing boards, which, to be frank, have traditionally made less-than-scintillating reading. How pleasantly surprised I was, then, to find *High-Impact Governing in a Nutshell* a thoroughly entertaining, quick read from beginning to end. You might not agree with every last conclusion that Doug draws or every bit of counsel he offers, but I promise that you will find his treatment of the extremely important subject of governing board leadership insightful, fresh, thought-provoking, and eminently practical. I know that you will want to keep it close at hand as one of your most precious resources as you move your board in the direction of higher-impact governance.

— Dr. William L. Minnix, Jr.
President and CEO
American Association of Homes and Services for the Aging

# Preface

For more than 20 years—at conferences, in workshops, and during intensive one- to two-day planning retreats—I have talked with thousands of nonprofit and public board members, CEOs, and senior managers about the in's and out's of governing board leadership and the board–CEO working relationship. During these two decades, participants in my sessions have repeatedly raised certain questions. *High-Impact Governing in a Nutshell* is organized around 17 of these oft-asked questions. My answers provide a very practical, down-to-earth guidebook filled with real-world guidance that you can put to good use in developing the capacity of your board to produce the kind of high-impact governing that associations and other nonprofit and public organizations need in these always changing and challenging times. You will also find *High-Impact Governing in a Nutshell* to be a powerful resource in building a close, productive board–CEO partnership that can withstand crises and the inevitable day-to-day stresses and strains that every organization experiences.

Whether you are a prospective or current board member, a CEO, or a senior manager, you can put the hands-on guidance that you will find in this guidebook to immediate use in your organization, whether it is an association or other nonprofit or public organization. The wisdom that I share in the following pages was primarily learned in the trenches, working with nearly 500 nonprofit and public organizations of every conceivable shape and size—including many associations—providing services in such fields as education, health care, public transportation, economic and community development, social services, and historic preservation. Tested and refined in actual practice, the advice and counsel you will find in *High-Impact Governing in a Nutshell* will arm you to develop truly high-impact governing boards that make a real difference in the affairs of your organization, building on the foundation of solid board–CEO partnerships that can stand the test of time.

*High-Impact Governing in a Nutshell* is a relatively brief guidebook that cannot serve as your definitive resource in the incredibly complex field of nonprofit and public governance. Even though it deals with many of the most important and complex questions related to board leadership, you are well advised to dig into the rapidly growing governance literature more deeply in your quest to become ever more "board savvy." And keep in mind that *High-Impact Governing in a Nutshell* is not intended to be a beginners' manual. Rather, it is aimed at readers who have already mastered the governing basics, such as how to put together an effective meeting agenda, and who are now ready to move to the next level in developing the board's capacity to do truly high-impact governing.

# Acknowledgements

I am indebted to the board members and CEOs of the hundreds of nonprofit organizations that I have worked with over the past quarter-century for providing me with the opportunity to acquire the experience that is at the heart of *High-Impact Governing in a Nutshell*. In a very real sense, these board members and CEOs have been my teachers as well as esteemed colleagues, and I am in their debt for the wisdom they shared and the lessons they taught.

This is the fourth book that I have written for the American Society of Association Executives (ASAE), beginning with *Boards That Work* in 1995. I highly value my long-standing professional association with ASAE and greatly respect the role that this stellar organization has played in advancing the art and science of non-profit leadership and management. I want to thank Baron Williams, Director, Book Publishing and Sales, and Janice Dluzynski, Director, Information/CEO Central, for their encouragement and support during the preparation of the manuscript. I also want to thank Greta Kotler, Senior Vice President of Professional Development and Credentialing, and Jamie Sadler, Director of Learning Experiences, for the opportunity to discuss many of the key concepts in this book with association executives in educational programs sponsored by ASAE, as well as Keith Skillman, Editor-In-Chief of *Association Management*, for encouraging me to experiment with new ways to describe the concepts in writing.

A number of association CEOs devoted precious time to reviewing the conceptual outline and early chapters of this book and provided me with very insightful and practical suggestions for making *High-Impact Governing in a Nutshell* a more powerful resource for nonprofit leaders. In this regard, I want to thank: John Balance, Executive Director of the Materials Research Society; Gregory Balestrero, President & CEO of the Project Management

Institute; Jackie Barnes, Interim CEO of Girl Scouts of the USA; Robert Betz, Executive Director of the Health Industry Group Purchasing Association; Thomas Bowman, President & CEO of the Association for Investment Management and Research; Linda Chreno, Executive Vice President of the Florida Society of Association Executives; Ken Crerar, President & CEO of the Council of Insurance Agents and Brokers; Michael Davis, CEO of the American Alliance for Health, Physical Education, Recreation and Dance; Arthur Goessel, Executive Director of Independent Accountants International; Paul Houston, Executive Director of the American Association of School Administrators; and James Morley, President of the National Association of College and University Business Officers. Other executives who deserve my thanks for their thoughtful suggestions are: Deborah Atkinson, Director of Training, NISH; and Harry Capell, Rick Martino, and Carmen Rivera, respectively Senior Vice President, Volunteer and Chapter Support, Senior Vice President, Human Resources, and National Training Director, March of Dimes.

In the Tampa Bay area Calvin Harris, Pinellas County Commissioner, Thomas Riggs, Chief Executive Officer of Directions for Mental Health, and Sue Spitz, CEO of The Spring of Tampa Bay, hosted luncheon roundtables at which nonprofit and public CEOs and executives commented on the early chapters of *High-Impact Governing in a Nutshell*. In this regard, I want to acknowledge the valuable input of: Steve Carroll; Susan Churuti; Marti Coulter; Sheff Crowder; Paul D'Agostino; Barbara Daire; Debbie Dawson; Paul Dietrich; Gloria Esteban; Jane Gallucci; Racine Hall; Suzanne Caltrider Horn; Gay Lancaster; Howard Latham; Susan Latvala; Carl Lavender; Sarah Macario; Gil Machin; Elizabeth McMahon; John Morroni; Grace Puterman; Joan Saunders; Karen Williams Seel; Steve Spratt; Alithia Stanfield; Robert Stewart; Jake Stowers; Pick Talley; Barbara Sheen Todd; Don Turnbaugh; Ava VanNahmen; Elizabeth Warren; Tom Wedekind; Kenneth Welch; Lynn Whitelaw; Mark Woodard; and Judy Yates.

Many of the key concepts in this book were developed—and a good deal of the drafting was done—while I was a guest at the home of my brother, William David Eadie, in that gem of a city, Portland, Oregon. My close and precious friendship with William, along with his frequent and generous hospitality, not only helped to make this a better book, but also made the writing task far less onerous.

As with earlier books of mine, my children Jennifer and William Eadie were valuable contributors, helping me to hone concepts and sharpen language. And I am indebted to my friend, professional collaborator, and wife, Barbara Carlson Krai, whose love, unwavering support, and constant encouragement made it possible for me to write this book while also managing the affairs of Doug Eadie & Company.

Although many contributors have made this a better book, I alone am accountable for any flaws that you might find.

— Doug Eadie
   Palm Harbor, Florida

# HOW CAN WE DEVELOP A HIGH-IMPACT GOVERNING BOARD?

## HIGH-IMPACT BOARDS

A truly high-impact governing board makes a significant difference in the affairs of the nonprofit or public organization it is responsible for governing, whether it is a national association, a hospital, a public transportation agency, or any other member of the huge and diverse family of nonprofit and public organizations. If a high-impact board were to disappear overnight, it would be sorely missed because of the major contribution it regularly makes to organizational success and well-being. Signs indicating that a high-impact board is at work in a nonprofit or public organization include: clear, detailed values and vision statements, strategic directions, and policies; sufficient financial resources that are rationally allocated to programs, within the framework of a clear mission statement; a firm grasp of financial and operational performance; and a positive public image, among others.

Among the most important characteristics that the high-impact boards I have observed over the past 20 years have had in common are:

- their focus on their governing work above all else, never letting non-governing activities interfere with their primary governing mission

- the proactive, generative role they play in shaping the highest-impact governing "products," such as values and vision statements, and the consequent strong feeling of ownership that playing this role creates among board members

- the meticulous attention they pay to developing themselves as a human resource, making sure the board consists of qualified members whose governing skills are systematically developed

- their close, positive, enduring partnership with the chief executive officer (CEO) and the CEO's strong commitment to—and support of—the board's high-impact governing role

- the accountability they take for managing their own perform-ance as a governing body, setting clear, detailed performance targets and regularly assessing their governing performance

High-impact boards are not born, of course; they must be con-sciously and systematically developed, like any other organization, if they are to function at a high level. So, what is involved in develop-ing a nonprofit or public board into a high-impact governing body?

## AN ORGANIZATION BY ANY OTHER NAME...

Governing boards—situated at the pinnacle of the organizational pyramid, armed with ultimate authority over organizational affairs, and consisting of lay volunteers rather than employees—can seem different in kind from the other organizational units that make up your nonprofit or public organization: distant, aloof, and perhaps even a bit mysterious. However, you need to keep in mind that your board is, by definition, just an organization within the wider parent organization: a formally constituted group of people work-ing together through formal structure and process to achieve a common mission—in the case of a governing board: to govern. A governing board is, then, in form no different from a finance department or a member-services division.

## A CRITICAL CHOICE: DESIGN OR INHERIT

So what?—you might say. Well, if a board is an organization like any other organization, then it can be developed like any other organization to make it function more effectively and efficiently at carrying out its governing mission and doing its governing work. In fact, this brings us to one of the most critical choices you can make in the area of governance as a board member or CEO: Will you merely inherit the board of the past in terms of what you might call its "governing design," or will you tackle the job of systematically developing your board, helping it to become a higher-impact governing organization?

## THE SAD STATE OF AFFAIRS

You are probably saying to yourself, "That's a true no-brainer. Boards are too important, they have too much power, to leave to inheritance." However, the sad fact is that inheritance is still a very common choice where boards are concerned, and the systematic development of boards as governing organizations is still surprisingly rare. This is the reason why many boards, if not the majority, fall far short of their potential as governing bodies, providing far less strategic and policy direction and far weaker performance oversight than these challenging times demand. I am not sure what accounts for this sorry state of affairs, but my guess is that boards are still seen as largely an amateur undertaking—the province of lay volunteers rather than full-time professional managers—and as falling into a political realm that is less amenable to rational development. One of the greatest ironies in the field of nonprofit and public management is that boards, while they in theory are positioned at the pinnacle of the organizational pyramid, have been so under-designed and under-managed.

Without question, the work of governing boards has received far less attention than executive-management functions in the field of leadership and management. You can easily prove this by walking into any major bookstore and asking to see the books on boards. I promise that you will be lucky to find four or five books dealing with governance, three of those will probably be outdated, and none will focus on nonprofit or public boards. Ask to see the books on executive leadership and management, however, and you will find the shelves filled with choices.

## THE ESSENTIALS OF BOARD DEVELOPMENT

The point of developing your board is to strengthen its capacity to do its work—which is to govern your nonprofit or public organization—more effectively and efficiently. The 16 other questions that I address in the following pages largely relate to board development, which involves updating what I call your board's "governing design," which consists of the following key elements:

- **Developing the people on your board**
  What should the composition of your board be, in terms of such factors as gender, race, and professional or industrial affiliation? What attributes and qualifications should your board look for in new board members? What steps should your board take to influence the filling of board vacancies to ensure that you achieve the desired composition and find the desired attributes and qualifications? What steps should your board take to strengthen its members' governing skills?

- **Developing the work of your board**
  What elements should make up your board's "governing mission"? What governing decisions should your board make about what "governing products" (e.g.,updated vision and mission statements; the annual budget) on a regular basis, and how should your board go about making these decisions? What governing products should basically be developed by staff and reviewed by the board, and what products should your board play a more proactive and creative role in generating? What non-governing work should your board be doing?

- **Developing the structure of your board**
  How large should your board be? What process should be employed for electing or appointing board members? How often should your board meet? What standing committees should your board employ in doing its work?

## APPROACHES TO BOARD DEVELOPMENT

Unless you are present at the creation of a new association or any other nonprofit or public organization, the proverbial train is running, and your governing board is already doing its work according to an existing organizational design that answers the foregoing questions about the people, the work, and the structure. Realistically speaking, your board's governing design is probably working generally well and does not require wholesale reform (which as you have no doubt learned tends to fail, anyway). Therefore, more often than not, we are talking about incrementally updating selected pieces of the design. For example, you might decide to expand the number of board seats by three to promote greater diversity, to fine-tune the committee structure to make it a more effective governing vehicle, or to upgrade the board's role in strategic decision making by adding to your planning cycle an annual board–staff retreat focusing on the identification of strategic issues.

The process of board organizational development is never-ending, of course, because you will always want to take advantage of advances in the field of nonprofit and public governance to strengthen board performance. The need for continuous improvement in the board "business" has been successfully addressed in a number of ways. For example, many boards have assigned responsibility for board organizational development to an "executive" or "governance" committee, which is expected to recommend governing improvements to the full board as appropriate. Many boards reserve a half-day of their annual $1\frac{1}{2}$- to two-day planning retreat for identifying practical ways to strengthen board performance. And when the organizational design of a board has not been updated for several years, resulting in dramatic board underperformance, it might make sense for a board to create an ad hoc "governance task force" to spend several weeks, or even months, to identify needed updates to the board design.

### EXPECT RESISTANCE

You are well advised to expect some—perhaps a lot of—resistance when you get involved in tinkering with the organizational design of your board, for two key reasons. First, many, if not most, of the members of the board might feel pretty satisfied with their governing performance, even though you can see a major gap between the board's governing potential and its actual performance. After all, many board members have neither the time nor the interest to keep up with new thinking in the field of nonprofit and public governance; indeed, many incoming board members have scant knowledge and experience in governing. Second, and probably more important, board members frequently feel strong ownership of particular elements of the current organizational design.

For example, I recently worked with a nonprofit association board that was saddled with a badly designed standing-committee structure that was seriously impeding board governing perform-ance. The existing structure of "silo" committees (e.g., member services, education and training, annual conference) divided the board's attention into narrow chunks that were more related to program administration than governance and turned the board into a collection of technical advisory committees and, even worse, board members into ardent program advocates. The need for broader functional committees with a governing focus (e.g., plan-ning and development, performance monitoring) was pressing, as the association's ad hoc governance task force pointed out in its report at the end of an intensive four-month process.

Although the task force made a compelling case for re-structuring the board's committees, two long-tenured board members chairing existing silo committees put up a strong fight against reform. It was clear to me, as an external observer, that their opposition had little to do with the merits of the case. Rather, it was ego at work. In my mind, I could hear them saying: "I've devoted hundreds of hours over the years learning to work with the existing structure, and finally, now that all of my hard work has resulted in my chairing this committee and at long last exerting significant influence as a board member, you are telling me we need a new structure, which will take away my influence in one fell swoop. Not on your life!"

The surest way to overcome resistance to updating your board's organizational design is to involve as many board members as feasible in coming up with the enhancements, thereby building board-member ownership of the proposed changes. You want to make sure, as well, that powerful, "old guard" board members are involved in developing the improvements, rather than being left on the sidelines to take pot shots at the recommended reforms.

# CHAPTER 2

# WHAT IS THE CEO'S ROLE IN BOARD DEVELOPMENT?

## THE PRIME MOVER

Since strong, creative board leadership is one of the preeminent keys to your association's long-term success in this changing, challenging world, board capacity building must be on the top-five list of your CEO, who is by virtue of position a major league player in the governance game. Any CEO (and I hear this every now and then) who sits back bemoaning the board's lackluster leadership without taking affirmative action to help the board become a higher-impact governing body is guilty of dereliction of duty—and of being less than a full-fledged CEO. Behind every truly high-impact governing board that I've ever seen has always been a CEO who

- is passionately committed to strong board leadership,
- is dedicated to capitalizing on the board as a precious organizational asset,
- plays an active role in developing the board's governing capacity, and
- is what I call "boardsavvy."

Indeed, in my experience, the CEO must be not just an active participant in but also the prime mover of board development, playing the leading—not just supporting—role in helping the board realize its tremendous governing promise in practice. The reasons are obvious. As part-time volunteers who spend the bulk of their time living busy lives outside of the board, your board members couldn't realistically be expected to muster the time and energy required to keep up with the rapidly changing field of nonprofit governance, much less attempt to get the board-development job done on their own.

Being the prime mover of board capacity building doesn't mean that the CEO takes command of the development process publicly, visibly leading board members by the nose through the process. On the contrary, truly "board-savvy" CEOs spend quite a bit of their time in the board-development arena leading from behind, making sure that board members themselves are visibly involved in fashioning board-development strategies and getting board members to play public leadership roles in implementing the strategies. They fully understand that board members aren't likely to be strongly committed to the steps involved in moving toward higher-impact governing (for example, implementing a more effective standing-committee structure) unless they feel strong ownership of the process, which depends on their in-depth, visible involvement every step of the way.

By the way, I use the term "CEO" to describe the highest ranking, full-time professional in your nonprofit organization, who is appointed by—and accountable directly to—the board, and who is responsible for all internal operations of your organization. The increasingly common title for CEO in the nonprofit world (and universally in for-profit corporations) is "president and CEO," although you will still find the somewhat misleading and anachronistic titles—"executive director" and even (in associations) "executive vice president"—floating around in the nonprofit world. The chief-executive function cannot by its very nature be shared with the board chair or any other association board member, at least not without diluting CEO accountability and seriously weakening the CEO's position.

## AN EMERGING NEW MODEL OF "CEOSHIP"

As I've traveled around the country working with and observing hundreds of CEOs over the past 20 years, I've seen a new breed of CEO emerging whose leadership style makes them far more effective at building partnerships with their boards than the command-and-control bosses of yore:

- These modern CEOs see themselves as more than merely the top professional serving as the link between the board and professional staff. In their view, the CEO is a hybrid position, part board member and part staff member. Board members are colleagues and peers, not just the boss, of the modern CEO, who more frequently these days actually sits on the board (although not typically as a voting member). In a sense this view of the CEO role is the product of a maturation process, as the nonprofit corporate sector moves closer to its for-profit counterpart.

- The modern CEO sees himself or herself as preeminently a capacity builder, primarily responsible for helping every part of the organization to realize its leadership and management potential as fully as possible. In this regard, the modern CEO thinks like an architect and designer, devoting considerable time and attention to making sure that the individual components of the organization (e.g., the board, the executive team, such systems as strategic planning and budgeting) are well designed—taking advantage of advances in the field of leadership and management—and that they are appropriately linked (e.g., the board is creatively and proactively involved in the strategic-planning process).

- The modern CEO pays close attention to the psychological and emotional dimension of leadership, capitalizing on every opportunity to build feelings of ownership and ego satisfaction among both board members and executives. Therefore, the modern CEO spends little time giving orders, instead playing the facilitator role, assisting board and staff members to participate effectively in organizational processes such as strategic planning and more often than not leading from behind rather than up-front.

## AN AFFIRMATIVE APPROACH

In my experience, the nonprofit CEOs whose boards become truly high-impact governing bodies and whose partnerships with their boards are close, productive, and enduring, without exception, bring a fundamentally positive attitude to the governing game. This doesn't mean that they are cockeyed optimists who see everything through rose-colored glasses, but it does mean that when they look at their board, they see a precious asset to be developed and exploited in the interest of strong governance.

These CEOs are not captives of what I call the "damage-control" mind-set where their boards are concerned, and they are not preoccupied with fashioning an elaborate structure of policies (rules) that are aimed at protecting executive prerogatives from board meddling. Instead of approaching the board from a defensive posture, pondering how to protect themselves and their staff from board incursions into administrative matters, these CEOs ask themselves from the get-go: "What can I do to help my board members realize their tremendous governing potential so that my association is well governed?"

The CEO of a trade association in the health field taught me a leadership technique that had served her well in working with her board for nearly a decade and that demonstrates a powerful constructive attitude at work. "I think of my CEO job," she said, "as falling into two main parts. Of course, as CEO, I'm accountable to my board for all operations of the association, and I should be rewarded and punished on the basis of the programmatic and financial targets that the board and I have agreed to. But in addition to being responsible for the whole shebang, I serve as 'executive director' of a particular 'program'—my board—and in this capacity I'm explicitly accountable for making sure my board is really effective at governing and that my board members find deep satisfaction in governing. I spend lots of time thinking about my board's developmental needs, I set specific board-development targets, and I strategize ways to get my chair and other board members committed to developing themselves."

## BOARD-SAVVY CEOS

Being a "board-savvy" CEO above all else means you are a real expert in the governing "business," knowing it inside-out and keeping abreast of advances in this rapidly changing field. Otherwise you can't expect to play the leading role in board development. Board-savvy CEOs don't fall victim to fallacious "little golden rules" offered with scientific certitude—such as the classic bit of bad counsel that "small boards are better"—nor are they customers for heavily hyped one-size-fits-all governing models. They make a serious and continuous effort to develop what I call their "governing IQ" through in-depth reading and participation in educational programs. For example, many nonprofit CEOs are members of BoardSource (formerly the National Center for Nonprofit Boards), a national nonprofit membership organization that is a comprehensive source of publications dealing with the basic functions of governing boards. Over the years, BoardSource has developed an extensive library of materials on every facet of governing-board operations, such as the board's hiring and evaluation of the CEO and the board's role in planning and monitoring performance

Board-savvy CEOs also take advantage of the growing body of publications on governance of national and state professional and trade associations representing particular nonprofit sectors such as health care, education, and association management (e.g.,the American Hospital Association, the American Association of Homes and Services for the Aging, the American Association of School Administrators, the American Association of Community Colleges, and the American Society of Association Executives). Many association magazines and journals these days regularly publish articles that feature real-life accounts of successful experience in building governing capacity. And certain associations have been formed specifically to represent the special interests of governing boards, for example, the National School Boards Association (NSBA), the Association of Governing Boards (AGB), and the Association of Community College Trustees (ACCT). Association magazine articles are not only a good way to keep track of practical experiments in board building, they can also keep you abreast of current debates in the field, acquainting you with competing viewpoints on such matters as the use of standing committees and optimum board size.

Associations and publishing houses such as Jones & Bartlett and Jossey-Bass are increasingly publishing books that deal with nonprofit governance, a trend that has undoubtedly been accelerated by highly public scandals in for-profit governance, such as the Enron disaster. To develop and maintain your governing IQ, you are well advised to build a library of books on nonprofit governance and to put them high on your professional reading list. Probably the best way to build your nonprofit governance library is to consult the catalogs of major nonprofit publishers and national and state associations. Many association catalogues feature mainline nonprofit governance books that go beyond the boundaries of the particular profession or trade the association represents. For example, my *Extraordinary Board Leadership* is carried in the publications catalog of the American Association of Homes and Services for the Aging.

## BEING A CAUTIOUS CONSUMER

As you read comprehensive works on nonprofit boards, you should be a cautious consumer, keeping in mind, first, that the "field" of nonprofit governance involves far more art than science, and, second, that writers have been known to espouse dubious conventional wisdom with misleading and dangerous certitude. As a general rule, I recommend that you approach your reading in the governance arena with a healthy sense of skepticism, paying special attention to uncovering the assumptions that underlie whatever advice is being proffered, as well as continuously comparing what you are reading with your real-life experience in working with boards. As a cautious consumer of governance literature, you will want to be especially suspicious of any approach to the work of nonprofit governing boards that claims to be a comprehensive, one-size-fits-all "model." Too much neatness and order should ring your internal alarm bells, alerting you to the possibility of being sold a bill of goods. Here are three key questions that I always ask when I pick up a new book on boards:

1. What are the sources of the author's wisdom? Is he or she drawing on substantial direct experience in working with a wide variety of nonprofit boards, or is he or she taking a more academic approach, merely summarizing the work of writers? While there is some value in summarizing the research of others, you have good reason to be skeptical of any book that offers primarily second-hand advice.

2. What fundamental attitudes about the work of nonprofit governing boards have shaped the book's content? If the author basically sees his or her mission as helping you keep the board well under control and out of the business of executive

management and administration, then you will probably find a heavy emphasis on fashioning elaborate "policies" (essentially rules) aimed at distinguishing between board and executive functions. On the other hand, if an author sees the board as essentially a precious asset to be put to work on behalf of the nonprofit, then you are likely to find close attention being paid to practical ways of involving the board creatively in key processes such as strategic decision making.

3. How balanced and comprehensive is the author's approach to the subject of governing board leadership? For example, does he or she address every key element of what I call the "governing design:" the role and work of the board; the processes for involving the board in doing that work, such as operational planning/budget preparation and strategic decision making; the development and management of the board as a human resource (e.g., how to ensure more qualified board members and how to develop governing skills); and the structural dimension (e.g., use of standing committees, the role of the executive committee in board management)? Or does the author attempt to hard sell a "model" that is too neat and boilerplate to adequately capture the complexity of the governing "business"?

# WHAT DOES IT MEAN TO "GOVERN"?

## MUCH MORE THAN POLICY MAKING

One of the key characteristics of what I call "high-impact" governing boards is that they concentrate on their governing work. So what does it mean to "govern"? I have interviewed thousands of nonprofit and public board members over the years, preparing for planning retreats and gathering information for books and articles. One of the first questions I always ask is: "Would you please explain—in a nutshell—what you and your colleagues on the board do when you are governing? What, in essence, is the work of governing?" Now, you might think that answering this straightforward question would be a piece of cake to most board members, or at least those who have spent a year or more on the board, but you would be wrong. Fully half of the board members I have interviewed have initially responded with stunned silence, and if I have heard once, I have heard a thousand times: "What an interesting question! Give me a couple of minutes to think about that." More often than not, the answer, when it finally comes, does not go much beyond the familiar mantra that governing means "making policies that the CEO and staff carry out."

If you think about it for more than a couple of minutes, it will be as obvious to you as it is to me that policy making alone could not keep a board very busy for long. After all, what is a policy but a broad rule to govern one aspect or another of your organization's operations? Some policies are truly high level and involve significant stakes; for example, determining how contractual commitments can be made, how large a check the CEO can sign without explicit board approval, the management compensation structure, or professional certification requirements. The great majority of policies in any organization are essentially operational in nature and would never come to the attention of a governing board. The point is, once the major policies of an organization have been formulated and adopted by the board, they only need to be updated periodically. Where is the governing meat in policy making? There is very little, which is why making policies could not possibly keep a governing board gainfully employed.

## A FULLER DEFINITION OF GOVERNING

Some three years ago, in the process of writing the book, *Extraordinary Board Leadership: The Seven Keys to High-Impact Governance*, I devoted several hours to coming up with an updated definition of "governing" that reflected what I had learned over the years in working with hundreds of high-impact governing boards. I finally came up with a general definition of the work of governing that satisfied me in the sense that it matched my real-life experience. Subsequently, I have run this definition by many board members and CEOs, the great majority of whom have agreed that it fits the bill. Here it is:

**To govern means to play the leading role—in partnership with the CEO and senior managers—in continuously answering three fundamental questions, thereby determining the shape and course of the organization:**

1. **Where should our organization be headed and what should it become over the long run?**
2. **What should our organization be now and in the near future?**
3. **How well is our organization performing—programmatically, financially, and administratively?**

Keep in mind that this definition covers only the preeminent work of a governing board, which is obviously to govern. I think that a strong case can be made for board involvement in such non-governing work as raising money and building ties to key stakeholders in the external world, as you will see later. But for now, I want to focus on the governing job for the very compelling reason that your organization's success and welfare depend heavily on your board doing this critical job in a full and timely fashion.

## FLESHING OUT THE DEFINITION

Three years ago, armed with a general definition of governing that adequately described what I observed high-impact boards regularly doing, I then asked myself what these governing boards actually did—in concrete detail—in the process of answering the three fundamental governing questions:

1. What governing judgments and decisions did these high-impact boards regularly make that significantly impacted the affairs of their organizations?

2. What kinds of governing "products" did these governing judgments and decisions relate to?

3. How involved were these high-impact governing boards in shaping and generating the governing "products" that they were regularly making judgments and decisions about?

4. And, finally, in shaping, generating, and making decisions about various governing products, how did these high-impact governing boards divvy up the labor with their CEOs and managers?

Now, even if the term "governing product" sounds a bit strange to you, bear with me, because only by getting down to the nitty-gritty level of product-like governing "chunks" can we really understand the process of governing, enabling us to teach and learn it. Otherwise, we can too easily get stuck in the la-la land of "policy making."

## FLESHING OUT THE GOVERNING PROCESS AND ROLES

Keep in mind that even though you can follow the models that high-impact governing boards have created in mapping out the work of your own nonprofit board, you will still have a pretty wide range of choice in deciding exactly what your board will do and when it will do it—in concert with the CEO and management staff—in accomplishing its governing work. You will recall that one of the characteristics of high-impact governing boards is that they play a proactive and generative role in shaping key governing products, and that they consequently feel strong ownership of their governing work. One of the major design choices every board, its CEO, and senior managers have regarding every governing product is how involved the board should be in shaping it: the deeper the involvement, the stronger the feelings of ownership.

I will be discussing the work of governing in quite a bit of detail in the following pages, but for now I want to look briefly at some examples that will clarify what I mean by governing "products" and the kinds of choices your board has in dealing with them. Let's start with the first key question that a governing board answers: Where should our organization be headed and what should it become over the long run? Answering that strategic question involves your board in regularly making decisions about such governing products as an updated values and vision statement, a list of strategic issues calling for attention, strategic goals, and so forth.

We tend to think of the strategic-planning process as the vehicle for getting decisions made about such critical governing products as values, vision, and strategic goals, but the field of strategic planning is highly complex and continuously changing, and so you have ample choice about how to reach these decisions. For example, there is the notoriously ineffective traditional approach: a consultant or staff develop a strategic-planning document containing an updated vision statement and send it to the board or one of its committees for review, thereby forcing board members to thumb through a finished document and preempting them from playing a creative role in shaping it. At the other end of the spectrum, higher-impact governing boards are likely to employ a strategic-planning retreat to kick off the planning process, at which—with CEO and management participation—a vision statement is roughed out through a brainstorming process and subsequently refined by the planning committee and adopted by the full board.

Let's take the second fundamental governing question: What should our organization be now and in the near future? Answering this question takes us to a more operational agenda, involving your board in making decisions about such operational products as your association's mission statement, its annual operating plan and budget, and operating policies of various kinds. Again, your board has ample choice in terms of its involvement in shaping and deciding about these more operational products. For example, no truly high-impact board that I have observed would ever get involved in working out the detailed numbers in the budget document, assigning dollars to specific objects of expenditure. However, many high-impact boards play a very creative, proactive role in shaping the major performance targets that are intended to guide development of the detailed financial document of their organization, and they devote close attention to possible, significant, new expenditures, for example, for a major new program or service.

And there is a creative role for your board in mapping the detailed governing work that is required to answer the third key governing question: How well is our organization doing—programmatically, financially, and administratively? Your board can certainly play a creative role—along with the CEO—in determining the performance indicators that should be monitored, the frequency and formats of reports, and the review process that will be employed. For example, many board performance-monitoring committees these days are requesting that creative graphics (such as bar charts) be used to report financial performance, such as comparing actual to budgeted expenditures by major organizational unit—year to date and for the current period.

In summary, the job of governing your nonprofit or public organization involves your board in regularly making decisions about particular governing products to answer four fundamental governing questions. The CEO and staff are necessarily involved in shaping and developing these governing products, and the precise division of labor—and depth of board involvement—are matters of choice. Although it makes good sense to follow the example of high-impact boards in mapping out your board's governing work, you will always have a number of specific design choices to make in determining precisely how to accomplish the governing work.

# CHAPTER 4

# WHAT IS THE IDEAL SIZE FOR A GOVERNING BOARD?

## MORE ART THAN SCIENCE

Working with hundreds of nonprofit and public boards over the past 20 years has taught me that there is more art than science involved in developing a governing board, and you are well advised to be skeptical whenever you come across one of those "little golden rules" that abound in the governance field, especially when you hear it espoused with scientific certainty. You owe it to yourself to be open in considering the pros and cons associated with advice you encounter in the governance arena, rather than jumping to premature conclusions and just uncritically going along with the advice. And when you consider the advice, make sure you understand what is really motivating the person offering it—what the core rationale is—which in my experience is often less-than-obvious on the surface.

This is certainly true when you are dealing with the question of board size, which is often the subject of heated debate and, believe it or not, considerable passion. One particularly misleading piece of conventional wisdom that I have heard authoritatively expounded over the years is that small boards (often defined as fewer than 15 members) are preferable to larger ones. This fallacious "little golden rule" has actually led many boards to reduce their effectiveness as governing bodies by engaging in needless and damaging downsizing. I am not suggesting that a board cannot conceivably be too large and unwieldy (I don't recommend going beyond 30 members at the outside), but I am encouraging you to think twice before sliding down the slippery slope of board downsizing without serious forethought.

Over the years, I have seen many more truly high-impact boards with more than 20 members than I have seen top-performing boards with fewer than 15 members. Is there an ideal size for a governing board? Obviously not in any scientific sense. However, I will say that a board in the range of 15 to 25 members works quite well in my experience, being small enough to manage and support relatively easily and large enough to bring significant benefits such as diversity and political influence.

## THE SMALL-BOARD CAMP

Passionate advocates of the simplistic, small-is-better position on board size typically approach the question from a negative perspective. Instead of exploring the connection between board size and governing capacity (e.g.,considering the benefits of greater diversity results from increasing the number of board seats), the small-board camp is dedicated to countering the purported evil effects of a mythical, bloated monster of a board that is too cumbersome to manage, at least in their eyes. These small-is-beautiful advocates are, when you get beyond the mythical monster they've created, essentially motivated by a narrow, uninspiring efficiency rationale that has a grain of truth to it. For example, they are surely correct that it is easier to assemble a quorum of an 11-member board than a 25-member board, but not so much easier, in my experience, that it really makes a significant difference.

I have also heard the argument from the small-board camp that it is easier to build a cohesive board "culture" when dealing with a smaller board. I concede that this is probably true, although in practice this all-too-often leads to what I call a "birds-of-a-feather" board with a contingent of look-alike and think-alike members. And, in my experience, many larger boards have successfully employed well-designed standing committees as a powerful tool for strengthening board culture.

## BIGGER IS BETTER

A board consisting of at least 15 members is preferable to a smaller board in three major ways:

First, you can achieve greater diversity. Diverse backgrounds, perspectives, experience, knowledge, and expertise are without question a major asset in making high-stakes strategic decisions and fashioning policies to deal with complex organizational matters. The more diverse the board, the more likely it will be to raise pertinent issues and questions and to avoid marching lock-step to disaster because of an ill-conceived and unchallenged course of action. In today's rapidly changing, challenging world, diversity—especially in terms of ethnicity and gender—is also a major cultural and political asset for any organization that needs and wants widespread public support.

Second, you can expand access to resources, including money and political support. Many larger boards these days are making sure that critical stakeholder organizations that are in a position to provide resources—for example, foundations, government agencies, and sister associations—are represented on the board. In fact, I have recently worked with several professional and trade associations that have set aside three to five seats on the board for "outside" directors who are not association members. In addition, many board members are actively participating in such external functions as speaking on behalf of their organizations in pertinent forums, testifying before legislative committees, and even lobbying with foundations on behalf of funding applications.

Third, you can achieve the critical mass that will enable your board to employ standing committees as powerful governing engines. I will discuss committees in greater depth later in this guidebook, but keep in mind that well-designed standing committees can make a major contribution to high-impact governing, principally by dividing the governing labor into manageable "chunks" that enable board members to delve more deeply into complex governing issues. Standing-committee work tends not only to strengthen governing decisions, but also to build feelings of satisfaction and ownership among board members.

## SO AVOID THE SMALL-BOARD TRAP

Without question, if your board is a precious asset, a larger board makes the best of sense—up to a point. I have suggested that you think in terms of a maximum of 25 board members, but in all honesty I have seen many truly high-impact governing bodies with 30 to 40 members. Of course, manageability of the governing process is a requirement, but you should not let yourself be seduced into believing that only a board of fewer than 15 members can be managed; experience has taught me that this just is not true. And as you think about the question of board size, just keep in mind that the benefits your association will realize from a board of at least 15 members easily outweigh the minor efficiency gains that a smaller board will produce. Of course, a larger board does involve costs, such as the staff time required to support board deliberations and the increased cost of reimbursing board members' travel to meetings. In my experience, however, the benefits of a larger board more than justify the added cost.

# CHAPTER 5

# WHAT CAN WE DO TO MAKE SURE THAT WE GET THE RIGHT PEOPLE TO FILL BOARD VACANCIES?

## THE KEY INGREDIENT IN HIGH-IMPACT GOVERNING

Far from being an abstract entity, your association's governing board is above all else the people serving on it, and your board members are without question the key ingredient in the high-impact governing recipe. The commitment, energy, intelligence, knowledge, and skills that your board members bring to the boardroom make your board an enormously precious asset. Of course, a well-designed governing "machine"—your board's structure and governing processes—make it possible to capitalize on that asset in generating the kind of high-impact governing decisions that these challenging times demand. But no matter how well designed the mechanics of your governing board are, the cast of characters making up the governing drama will always be a preeminent influence on the quality of your board's decisions. Therefore, it stands to reason that paying close attention to filling board vacancies is one of the wisest investments you can make in the governance arena.

As you probably know, the vast majority of nonprofit boards are self-appointing, which makes filling board vacancies a relatively straightforward process. By contrast, association boards are for the most part elected by the membership, or by one or more constituency bodies representing the membership, making the process of filling vacancies more complex—politically as well as technically. However, many boards with which I'm familiar—both of the self-appointing and elected variety—have strengthened their board's composition by taking three key steps:

1. Treat board human-resource development as a formal program for which a standing board committee is accountable.

2. As part of the board's human-resource development program, fashion and keep updated a detailed, two-part profile of the desired board in terms of composition and the attributes and qualifications of individual board members.

3. Employ this profile more or less directly in systematically influencing the filling of board vacancies.

## ADDED BENEFITS

Before we take a look at each of these three steps, I want to point out a couple of important benefits your association board will realize from taking its development as a human resource seriously, beyond the obvious one of ensuring that your board consists of the people you need to do high-impact governing work. One benefit that I've seen frequently over the years is heightened board self-esteem, which tends to deepen board members' commitment to their governing work. As far as I can tell, making board human-resource development a formal program with an accountable committee, and taking the trouble to fashion and use a detailed profile of the ideal board in terms of its members, tend to elevate the work of governing in the eyes of board members themselves, in a sense, solemnizing their governing work.

Knowing that your organization cares enough to ensure that the most qualified candidates fill board vacancies makes being on the board more of an honor and source of pride. We might not want to admit it, but ego satisfaction is an important ally of altruism in building feelings of commitment among the ambitious, high-achieving people who serve on boards.

When your board takes its own development as a human resource seriously, it also signals to your organization's membership, clients, customers, and important stakeholders in the wider world, such as sister associations that are potential partners and foundations that are a source of funding, that this is no ordinary board. Rather, your board's meticulous attention to its own human-resource development distinguishes it from the crowd, signaling that it is an extraordinary governing body well worth serving on and working with. Such recognition can turn your board into more of a magnet that attracts qualified candidates, as well as strengthening your organization's credibility in the eyes of stakeholders, including potential partners and funding sources.

## BEYOND THE OLD-TIME NOMINATING COMMITTEE

The most common tool for filling board vacancies is the traditional nominating committee, which is typically enshrined in a nonprofit organization's bylaws. The nominating committee's job is to recommend candidates to the membership for election or re-election to the board, and often officers as well. Some nominating committees are fairly closely held by their boards, which officially appoint nominating committee members. Others are more independent of board control—for example, elected by the association's membership or appointed by a third party, such as an assembly of delegates.

Regardless of what an organization's bylaws say about the nominating committee and the process of electing board members, in my experience, high-impact governing boards almost always take explicit accountability for influencing the process of filling board vacancies. This responsibility is often carried out through a formally established board human-resource development program that also includes the systematic development of board-member governing knowledge and skills (see Chapter 6). To ensure that this program is capably led and overseen, a standing committee is typically assigned accountability for the board human-resource development program. In my experience, it makes the best of sense for your board's executive committee (increasingly known as the governance committee) to take responsibility for the program, in light of its overall accountability for coordination of the board as a governing body (see Chapter 13 and Chapter 14).

In my professional opinion, there is no sound justification for an organization employing a nominating committee that is independent of the governing board's structure (e.g., elected by the members or composed of non-board chairs of non-board committees). Such independent nominating committees dilute the board's accountability for its governing performance by diminishing its influence over its own composition, while producing no serious benefit. In fact, the non-board, independent nominating committee tends, in my experience, to institutionalize paranoia, saying in effect: "If we don't keep the process of filling board seats out of the board's hands, those incumbents will hold on to power as long as they can, either directly by never leaving the board, or indirectly by rewarding their allies and supporters with board seats. The nominating committee is the best way to guard against the clear and present danger of self-aggrandizement."

I can only say that I have seen no convincing evidence of the self-aggrandizement that such independent nominating committees are intended to guard against. However, even if an independent committee is built into your nonprofit's bylaws, your board's executive (or governance) committee can still influence the election of board members, even if less directly, by developing the profile of the ideal board.

## COMPOSITION OF THE IDEAL BOARD

Your executive or governance committee's developing and annually updating a profile of the ideal board for your organization in terms of the people serving on it is one of your strongest tools for building your board's capacity to do high-impact governing work. The profile consists of two basic parts: (1) the board composition we're shooting for, in terms of board members' affiliations with particular demographic, social, and professional groups; and (2) the attributes and qualifications we're looking for in individual board members. Dealing with board composition obviously means addressing your board's diversity, forcing your executive committee to grapple with always complex and often controversial philosophical, ethical, political, and business development questions. One of the reasons we need a board is to deal with such issues, facing them squarely and making sure that we understand the consequences of particular answers.

So should our board's composition reflect the makeup of the wider community (or in the case of associations, the wider membership) in terms of gender? Race? Age? Or should we, with an eye to membership growth, make sure that our board's composition includes population segments we are hoping to attract to the association (e.g., women, African Americans, 20-somethings)? Although these questions have an ethical dimension, don't overlook the obvious business implications of diversification, for example, as a strategy for growing an association's membership. And keep in mind that many high-impact association boards have found that diversifying professionally can make the board's decision making more effective, especially in the area of strategic business development.

In this regard, I recently worked with a board that added two new members who brought significant experience in corporate mergers and acquisitions and entrepreneurial development, as part of a conscious business growth strategy. I have also seen nonprofit boards set aside seats for key stakeholder organizations in the quest for strategic partnerships. For example, one board I'm familiar with added the CEOs of two sister associations in the same industry, which laid the foundation for some highly successful joint ventures and eventually a merger with one of the sister associations.

## STRONG CASE FOR OUTSIDE BOARD MEMBERS

Diversifying your board's composition might require revision of your organization's bylaws, depending on their limitations. The classic case is an association whose board must consist solely of full-time professionals in the industry, trade, or profession that the association serves. As you probably know, this is a quite common feature of association bylaws and a strong enemy of diversity on the professional front. The rationale for such institutional narrow-mindedness can't possibly be good governance, since in-depth involvement in a profession or trade is not a prerequisite for governing. If it were, we'd have to restructure hundreds of thousands of for-profit and nonprofit boards—of hospitals, colleges and universities, school districts, economic development corporations, libraries, and the like. It is universally recognized in corporate America that experience and expertise outside an industry are critical to sound strategic decision making and to long-term competitiveness and growth.

Even though the case for diversifying your organization's board beyond just members engaged in a particular trade, profession, or industry is compelling from the perspective of high-impact governing, adding "outside" board members is often an emotionally charged issue. As far as I can tell, the emotion has to do with strong feelings of ownership, especially among founding mothers and fathers, who have often dedicated hundreds and hundreds of hours to climbing the association volunteer career ladder. Emotions run highest, in my experience, among those who have, through their association volunteering, actually helped shape a particular profession, including establishing professional performance standards and a credentialing process. These dedicated missionary types don't take lightly to outsiders tinkering with their precious association, and can be highly resistant to diversification of board membership.

In light of the potential for significant resistance, I recommend following the example of many high-impact association boards that have, in recent years, taken an incremental approach to diversification, for example, reserving 3 or 4 of 21 board seats for outside directors. Keep in mind that the smaller the board, the more difficult (if not impossible) the task of diversification; this is one of several sensible reasons why you wouldn't want to downsize your board to fewer than 15 seats (see Chapter 4).

## INDIVIDUAL ATTRIBUTES AND QUALIFICATIONS

Developing the profile of the ideal board also includes identifying the attributes and qualifications that you are looking for in individual board members. Of course, you can't expect any one person to embody all the desired traits, but it makes good sense to search for candidates that come close to the profile. The executive committee of an association I worked with a couple of years ago developed a profile that included such attributes and qualifications as: "strong commitment to our mission;" "successful experience on at least two other nonprofit boards;" "a team player;" "open-mindedness;" "demonstrated professional and/or business success;" "high ethical standards;" "ties to the corporation and/or foundation community."

## APPLYING THE PROFILE

The point of developing a profile of the ideal board for your organization in terms of its members is obviously to influence the election or appointment of board members who embody the profile, in the interest of your board doing higher-impact governing work. Your board's executive or nominating committee can obviously employ the profile in identifying and screening likely candidates to stand for election to the board, more or less directly depending on your association's bylaws. At the very least, your board's executive (or governance) committee can send the profile to the nominating committee and, if it isn't politically too risky, even suggest particular targets based on the profile. The governance committee of an association board I worked with a few years ago, for example, recommended to the nominating committee that it make a serious effort to find at least two female CEOs and an Asian-American to stand for election to the board.

Where individual traits are concerned, many high-impact boards—through either their executive or nominating committee—take the trouble to review resumes, conduct interviews, and even check references to determine how closely individuals match the desired attributes and qualifications. And even if your board can't directly do the screening through one of its committees, nothing prevents the board from recommending to the responsible body that such screening be done as part of the nominating process.

# CHAPTER 6

# HOW CAN WE PREPARE BOARD MEMBERS TO GOVERN EFFECTIVELY?

## GOOD NEWS–BAD NEWS

The better educated and trained your organization's board members are in the work of governing, the more likely they are to perform at a high level. So every board that is committed to high-impact governing must also be committed to its own continuing education, dealing with two basic educational challenges:

How can we make sure that new members joining our board are well prepared to hit the ground running, rather than spending their first year on the governing job learning the ropes?

How do we keep board members' governing knowledge and skills up-to-date so that they are able to participate productively and creatively in ongoing board capacity building?

The good news is that you couldn't ask for a better group of students than the people who populate your average nonprofit board. The great majority of board members whom I've observed over the years have been avid lifelong learners who are sincerely committed to doing a top-notch job of governing. This shouldn't come as any surprise, when you reflect on the kind of bright, high-achieving people who tend to make it to the boardroom. They are used to setting high standards and asking a lot of themselves, and they have already dedicated significant time and energy to acquiring the knowledge and skills that have contributed to their professional or business success. Slackers they are definitely not.

The "bad" news is that many if not most board members, in my experience, are at least initially reluctant to make much of an investment in developing their own governing knowledge and skills once they have gone through the basic orientation for new board members. This is really ironic when you think about the critical leadership role that we expect boards to play and their tremendous impact on organizational performance. That the very people who wouldn't blink an eye at investing handsomely in executive education are capable of questioning whether they should devote time and money to their own governing education is amazing, but all too often true. As far as I can tell, this is part misplaced altruism ("Programs and services have first claim on our limited dollars") and part ego ("At this point, having climbed so far up the professional ladder, I really can't see myself going back to school"). Whatever the cause, truly high-impact boards overcome the reluctance, recognizing that under-investing in developing their governing knowledge and skills is a classic penny-wise, pound-foolish course of action.

Nonprofit boards that I have seen deal with this twin educational challenge effectively have established a formal board-education process consisting of three elements: (1) a standing committee with overall responsibility for board education; (2) a thorough orientation program for incoming board members; and (3) a continuing education program aimed at keeping board member knowledge and skills current.

## THE EXECUTIVE OR GOVERNANCE COMMITTEE
Experience has taught me that if you want board members to pay close attention to a leadership function and really take it seriously, you will want to assign it to a board standing committee; otherwise you're unlikely to generate sufficient ownership and commitment to make it fly. This is what many association boards have done with the board-education function, which is typically made a responsibility of the executive—or what I prefer to be called governance— committee, in keeping with its overall role as the committee on board operations (see Chapter 13 and Chapter 14 for detailed descriptions of the executive/governance committee). In this capacity, the executive committee can:

- ensure that a formal board-education program addressing the twin challenges of new member orientation and continuing education is developed and annually updated—including setting clear goals, laying out a detailed work plan to achieve them, and committing the funds required to support the program.

- regularly monitor program performance and make adjustments as appropriate to produce stronger results.

## NEW-MEMBER ORIENTATION

One of the questions I always ask when interviewing board members is: "What does the board do to make sure that incoming members hit the ground running?" You might be surprised to learn that the answer is often "Nothing in particular." But even when the answer is "We provide new board members with an orientation," a little digging more often than not reveals that the orientation has little to do with the work of governing. Instead, new board members are often briefed in detail on the programs, services, budget, administrative structure, and other facets of organizational life with nary a word about the board itself.

Although you obviously want incoming board members to understand the key operational features of the organization they are being asked to govern, what they need more than anything else if they are to succeed at the governing business is a thorough orientation on the board itself. The need for this is now being widely recognized, and many organizations make sure that their orientation programs include such elements as the board's

- governing role (a formal governing mission if one exists),
- performance targets (what is expected of individual board members),
- committee structure: the roles and detailed responsibilities of the standing committees, and
- involvement points in such key processes as CEO evaluation, strategic planning, and budgeting.

Although you will still see CEOs handling the orientation of incoming board members, a growing practice is for members of the executive or governance committee to actually conduct the orientation themselves, as a means of visibly demonstrating that board education is a top priority, not just another job to be passed along to the CEO. Assigning the orientation job to committee members also reinforces the board's accountability for managing its own performance as governing body.

Another growing practice is formal mentoring: pairing each incoming member with a seasoned board member who plays a mentoring role for, say, the first six months of the new member's tenure. The mentor's major job is to make time available to discuss any questions the new board member has about the board and to provide coaching as appropriate.

## CONTINUING EDUCATION

Nonprofit governance is anything but a static field with hard and fast principles. Instead, every day that passes in this wild and wonderful (and relatively new) field sees yesterday's golden rules challenged, new principles proposed, and new approaches and techniques for generating higher-impact governance reported. Taking the time and effort to keep your board members abreast of developments in this exciting field can serve two important purposes. First, you can combat the fatigue, boredom, and even burnout that can work against high-impact governing—motivating, inspiring, and energizing your board members by raising their sights above the trenches where much of their governing work takes place.

Second, you can arm your board members with information that they can put to practical use in updating the board's governing design. For example, dramatic developments in the field of strategic planning (see Chapter 8) provide board members with opportunities to play a proactive, creative role in leading strategic change, rather than merely thumbing through a finished tome on its way to the proverbial dusty shelf.

Highly effective board continuing-education programs that I have observed over the years have included such elements as:

- a lending library of books and articles on governance that are regularly circulated among board members. In this regard, many associations have joined BoardSource (formerly the National Center for Nonprofit Boards), which publishes short, easy-to-read guidebooks covering every conceivable facet of governing-board operations. Busy board members are often more willing to read carefully selected articles than books, and it makes sense to have a staff member regularly review periodicals such as *Harvard Business Review* and ASAE's *Association Management*, looking for articles that will enrich board members' understanding of various aspects of their governing work. If the time is available, you might even have staff summarize articles so that board members can decide whether it's worth their while to read the whole thing.

- participation in educational programs addressing governance matters. Many associations retain consultants to present on-site educational programs for their board members exclusively, an approach that provides both stronger quality control and greater opportunity for in-depth participation—but at a price, of course. Many associations also encourage their board members to participate in governance programs offered at regional and national conferences. If board members finance their own travel, this can be a cost-effective option, but, if not, an on-site program might represent a more affordable option.

- building a half-day session on governance into the annual strategic-planning retreat, using this time to discuss recent advances in the field and to identify opportunities to fine-tune and strengthen governing structure and process.

Quality control is always a serious issue in the education business. It would obviously be counterproductive to send board members to a governance program that ends up being a sales pitch for one of those one-size-fits-all governing models that are always floating around. The most effective board continuing-education programs, in my experience, build quality control into the planning—often by asking the CEO to review potential educational offerings to ascertain if they are worth board members' time. Another issue is incentive to participate. Although board members are typically avid lifelong learners, they are also very busy people. Participation in educational programs will tend to increase, in my experience, if such participation is made a formal board member performance target (see Chapter 14).

# CHAPTER 7

# HOW CAN WE HELP OUR BOARD BECOME A COHESIVE GOVERNING TEAM?

## TEAMWORK AT A GLANCE

Teamwork in the abstract is neither here nor there. The only serious reason for developing your board's teamwork is to help it function as a more effective governing body that gets its governing work done more effectively and efficiently. The acid test of an effective team is its productivity in accomplishing its assigned tasks. Productive teams are also generally characterized by a high level of cooperation and coordination in getting their work done, harmonious relations among team members, the absence of debilitating conflicts, and the capacity to withstand considerable stress and strain without falling apart. You probably won't have any problem finding where your board belongs on the teamwork spectrum, between "herd of cats" at one end and "made in heaven" at the other.

Although it makes sense for your organization's board to pay focused attention to becoming a more effective governing team, you wouldn't want to carry teamwork too far. You obviously wouldn't want to attempt to eliminate all tension or even occasional conflict from your board's governing process. In today's changing, challenging world, which places a premium on your board's dealing with highly complex governing issues, the last thing you would want is a board of "good little boys and girls" who placidly go along with staff recommendations, without asking the really tough questions.

Tension is a given when intelligent, committed people grapple with challenging questions, and the more give-and-take in the decision-making process, the more effective the ultimate decisions are likely to be. Don't forget that one of the dangerous arguments you'll occasionally hear for a smaller, less diverse board is that it is "culturally more cohesive," which in practice, in my experience, is likely to mean too little debate and questioning, too few view-points, overly narrow perspectives—in short, a woefully inadequate decision-making process.

## BEATING THE ODDS

Turning a diverse group of 15 or more people with varied back-grounds, experience, expertise, and affiliations into a cohesive governing team can be a daunting task, especially in the association world. For one thing, direct interaction among association board members tends to be limited by the fact that the boards meet only quarterly, if not less frequently. Interaction tends to be even more limited when it takes place only in a formal board business meeting. In addition, the constituency representation mind-set that is such a strong part of the board's culture in many associations creates a centrifugal force that works against team building.

Imagine if the members of the Cleveland Indians thought of themselves as primarily accountable to particular groups of fans (e.g., those living west of the Cuyahoga River in Cleveland), rather than to each other as a team. Sounds ridiculous, doesn't it, as a game-winning strategy? But I have observed several association boards, many of whose members think of themselves as more accountable to segments of the membership (e.g., a regional asso-ciation board) than to their colleagues as a governing team.

In my experience, four strategies have proved most useful in building cohesive board-governing teams:

1. focusing on ultimate governing goals
2. employing a well-designed governing process and structure
3. following teamwork guidelines
4. building emotional bonds

## THE BOARD GOVERNING MISSION

Experience has probably taught you, as it has me, that members of a team tend to be more committed to their team's work when they clearly understand the ultimate purposes the team is intended to serve. There's no reason to believe that nonprofit boards are any exception, and, in fact, the ones I've observed that do have a handle on their governing purposes really do function as stronger governing teams. As I discuss in some detail in Chapter 1 and Chapter 3 earlier in this book, you can think of governing work in concrete terms as helping to shape, and making judgments and decisions about, such governing "products" as a values and vision statement for your association or an updated mission statement. However, you need to take a step above this to provide your board with a stronger sense of ultimate purpose, coming up with what I call the "Board Governing Mission."

As an organizational unit, it obviously makes sense for your board to have a mission statement, and many nonprofit boards have developed detailed governing missions to guide them in mapping out their detailed governing work and in developing their teamwork. I'm not talking about a two or three-sentence "pithy paragraph," but rather a detailed listing of the impacts/outcomes that the board's governing work is intended to produce over the long run. Many organizations have taken the approach of developing a preliminary governing mission statement in a retreat, then using a committee to refine it and ultimately adopting it by resolution. In the retreat setting, the first step in mission development can be accomplished by a brainstorming group that completes the sentence: "Our governing work is intended to produce the following long-term outcomes and impacts...."

The point is not that any board could achieve these outcomes by itself, but that they deserve significant time and attention from the board in carrying out its governing work, working with the CEO and executive team. For example, elements that have appeared in many nonprofit board governing missions include:

- a financially stable organization
- a diverse, growing revenue base
- steady membership growth

- well-conceived, planned, and executed programs that meet client (or member) needs
- significant innovation in response to a changing environment
- a clear vision for the future
- specific targets for diversification and growth in programs and services
- a close, productive, enduring relationship with the CEO

## GOVERNING PROCESS AND STRUCTURE

I've already dealt with the design of the governing process and structure in Chapter 1 and Chapter 3. Just keep in mind that strong teamwork skills—at least ones that last—cannot be developed in the abstract. Rather, they are primarily acquired by employing a well-designed governing process and structure in doing the board's governing work. The last thing you would want to do with your board is waste board members' time at an off-site team-building exercise, and then bring the board back to a real-life situation of a poorly designed governing process. I have seen this happen on more than one occasion, and the result is the opposite of team building: frustration, irritation, and even anger.

To take an example, several members of an association board I interviewed a few years ago shared their indignation at having participated in a two-day knockdown, drag-out, team-building retreat, which even included falling into each others' arms and leading each other around blindfolded in exercises designed to build trust and emotional bonding. The retreat did succeed in getting everyone thinking about teamwork, and it did generate a warm glow—no question. However, as I was informed, the glow quickly faded as the members of this association's board subsequently—back at the shop—participated in a poorly designed, strategic-planning process that involved board members at the tail-end, after strategies had already been fleshed out, leaving the board to thumb through finished documentation which it hadn't played a creative role in shaping. The feelings of being underused and treated as a passive audience quite effectively extinguished the glow, leaving only a bad taste.

## TEAMWORK GUIDELINES

Many organizations have found that putting together a set of simple, straightforward guidelines to govern board member interactions is an effective, inexpensive tool for strengthening board teamwork. A common approach is to develop the initial set of guidelines in a retreat setting, and after they have been refined and adopted, to update them every year or so. A national association's guidelines included, for example: "open, honest, frequent communication;" "respect for each other's viewpoints and opinions;" "no hidden agendas;" "support for the majority's decisions even if you disagree;" and "adherence to the formal governing structure and process established by the board."

Guidelines aren't worth the paper they're written on unless your board pays attention to their observance. In this regard, many association boards have assigned their executive (or governance) committee responsibility for monitoring board teamwork (see Chapter 14).

## EMOTIONAL BONDING

Strangers don't make good team members, and building greater intimacy among your board members is a proven way to grease the interaction wheels and help your board get through traumatic situations largely unscathed. Building emotional ties among association board members is a real challenge because of the limited amount of direct interaction, but many associations have successfully narrowed the distance among board members by taking such simple steps as:

- asking every board member to supply a detailed biographical sketch, covering both professional and personal details, and putting the sketches together in a handbook distributed to all board members
- adding informal social interaction to regular board business meetings, for example, over lunch or dinner and at such special events as an evening river cruise or attendance at a sporting event

- holding an annual one- to two-day retreat away from head-quarters, with considerable breakout-group work built in as a means to foster active interaction

- employing standing committees of the board as a way to strengthen interaction through small-group work involving less formality than full board meetings

# CHAPTER 8

# HOW CAN OUR BOARD PARTICIPATE IN A MEANINGFUL WAY IN STRATEGIC PLANNING?

## MEETING THE CHANGE CHALLENGE

Your nonprofit organization, like all other organizations and institutions, has a choice in today's changing, challenging world. You can build the capacity to lead and manage your own change—proactively and creatively—in response to the changing world around you, fashioning and executing strategies to capitalize on opportunities and to avert threats. Or you can circle the wagons in hopes of protecting your organization's status quo from the changes swirling around you. The siren song of comfort and security will always tempt people to go on the defensive in the face of change, but you know there's not really a choice.

Your organization's long-term survival and growth depend on its mastering the change challenge. Merely defending yourself would be a recipe for sure decline, and perhaps even extinction if the changes around you are truly strategic (e.g., rapid consolidation in your industry that is taking a huge toll on your association's membership;or a sister nonprofit with abundant resources going after a large chunk of your market).

Keep in mind that your organization can deal with the never-ending change challenge at two levels, concurrently traveling along two very different but parallel planning and management tracks. The track that we're all most comfortable with is what I think of as "running the shop," which involves incrementally refining and adjusting programs, services, and administrative practices through the annual operational-planning and budget-preparation process. In my experience the great majority of associations and other nonprofit organizations have thoroughly mastered the techniques of managing what is, and, consequently, considerable incremental change gets accomplished through the tried-and-true operational planning and budgeting process,

The other track—leading and managing *strategic* change—is another matter entirely. Now we're venturing onto far less familiar and comfortable terrain, where we must deal with much more complex, higher-stakes issues (in the form of both challenges and opportunities) that demand more of a response from our organization than merely refining and updating our existing programs, services, and practices. This is far more difficult terrain, not only technically speaking, but also because larger-scale change is emotionally so challenging to human beings, which is why, in the words of Dr. Scott Peck, it tends to be the "road less traveled." This is the territory of what has traditionally been called "strategic planning."

## A SORDID HISTORY

I tend to avoid the term "strategic planning" in my work for two reasons. First, there is no such thing as *the* strategic planning process; it tends to mean a hundred different things to a hundred different people. Second, the process as traditionally applied has, over the years, earned a deserved reputation for ineffectiveness as a tool for leading strategic change. In a nutshell, the problem with traditional strategic planning—sometimes called comprehensive long-range planning—is that it has tended to project everything an organization is already doing into the future, often for a meaningless, totally arbitrary period such as three or five years. This approach has tended to generate bloated compilations of the conventional wisdom that eventually make their way to dusty shelves, where they reside—largely forgotten and virtually never consulted.

Strategic planning in its comprehensive long-range planning form has failed miserably as a tool for dealing with strategic change. For one thing, focusing on everything already going on in an organization inevitably buries people in detail, making it extremely difficult to focus on complex change challenges (strategic issues) that don't fit into current programmatic and administrative compartments. For another, in a rapidly changing world, projecting, in detail, an organization five years into the future (or any other meaningless period) is a monumental waste of time. We can't possibly forecast with any precision what our world will be like five years hence.

Fortunately, in recent years, a variation on the broad strategic-planning theme that is explicitly intended to deal with strategic change has been developed and thoroughly tested: the "Strategic Change Portfolio." At last we have a very powerful vehicle for involving your board creatively and proactively in leading strategic change.

## THE PORTFOLIO APPROACH AT A GLANCE

The strategic change portfolio is essentially a "holding pen" for strategic projects—often called strategic change initiatives—that have been developed to address particular strategic issues that an organization's board and CEO have selected for immediate attention. Each of these initiatives, or projects, consists of the goals to be achieved, implementation strategies, and the implementation revenue/expenditure budget. At any given time, the strategic change initiatives in the portfolio will involve a range of time frames. For example, Initiative A—effecting a merger with a sister association—will require 18 months for implementation; Initiative B—the image-enhancement campaign—will require 9 months; Initiative C— major revamping of the annual conference—will take 12 months; and Initiative D—restructuring of the board's standing committees— will take 6 months. As initiatives are implemented, they move from the portfolio to mainstream operations, and new initiatives take their place as new strategic issues are identified and selected.

The real power of the strategic change portfolio approach lies in its focus on a small number of issues that the board and CEO have decided: (1) demand immediate attention because of the stakes involved and the prohibitive cost of deferring action; and (2) cannot effectively and/or safely be handled through the mainstream operational-planning/budget-preparation process. The governing rule is that if an issue can, indeed, be effectively addressed through the annual operational-planning process, then it should be. The steps involved in developing the portfolio are:

- updating your organization's detailed vision for the future, in terms of its intended long-term impacts on the environment generally and its members or clients more specifically and its role and scope of activities

- identifying major issues in the form of challenges and opportunities by scanning the external environment and assessing internal strengths and weaknesses. An issue is defined as an opportunity to move closer to your organization's vision or a challenge standing in the way of movement toward the vision.

- selecting the issues that are sufficiently strategic to merit immediate attention

- fashioning the strategic change initiatives to address the selected issues

## THE GOLD STANDARD

Two compelling reasons dictate that your organization's board be involved in a creative, proactive fashion in the strategic change portfolio process, making it the gold standard for board participation in the affairs of your organization:

- Your board is uniquely qualified to participate in the process of identifying and selecting strategic issues, which benefits tremendously from the diverse experience, expertise, knowledge, and perspectives that your board members bring to the table.

- Psychologically speaking, your board's creative and proactive involvement in such a high-stakes, high-impact process is one of the surest ways to build board member satisfaction and commitment. Indeed, leaving your board on the periphery of the action in the portfolio process is a surefire way to breed frustration and erode commitment among board members.

## CREATIVE AND PROACTIVE INVOLVEMENT

In my experience, organizations that have realized the strongest return on their board members' involvement in the strategic change portfolio process—in terms of both leading and managing strategic change and board-member satisfaction and enthusiasm—have involved their board members intensively early in the process: in updating the organization's vision statement and identifying and selecting the strategic issues to be addressed. Once the issues have been selected, the process of developing the detailed action strategies that make up the initiatives is essentially a staff job.

A common, highly effective approach is for the whole board to meet with its CEO and executive managers in an annual retreat (sometimes called "strategic work session"), at which a rough cut of the updated vision statement is generated, a preliminary set of strategic issues are brainstormed, and possible strategic change initiatives are discussed. The board's planning committee, working closely with the CEO and executive team, then follows up by fine-tuning the vision statement, which is subsequently adopted by the full board, and by analyzing and refining the list of strategic issues, which is eventually approved by the board. From this point on, detailed development of the strategic change initiatives is handled by staff, perhaps with consulting assistance and non-board volunteer involvement in one or more task forces.

# CHAPTER 9

# HOW CAN WE INVOLVE OUR BOARD IN IMPLEMENTING STRATEGIC CHANGE?

## DAUNTING ODDS

Let's say that the strategic change initiatives making up your organization's current strategic change portfolio have been meticulously developed. The action strategies are technically and politically sound, and the budgets are realistic. You're home free, and implementation will be a piece of cake, right? Not really. The sad fact is that significant planned change is notoriously difficult to achieve. And even when it does get accomplished, the implementation process seldom goes smoothly and quite often causes a fair amount of pain and suffering for everyone involved. No matter how well developed the strategic change initiatives in your organization's strategic change portfolio might be, they are not self-implementing, and good planning is no more than half the battle.

Although always-scarce resources and the inexorable press of day-to-day operations obviously work against the timely implementation of strategic change, the real enemy is normal human resistance. The fact is, people generally dislike change when it touches directly on their work and lives. For one thing, significant change tends to force people out of their comfort zone, conjuring up the possibility of failure and public embarrassment, which outranks fear of death 10 to 1. I've met many more people over the years who would rather put up with mild boredom and reduced expectations than venture very far into uncharted terrain that feels dangerous. "Sure, it falls far short of perfect, but at least I know it well," is an all-too-common refrain.

Another powerful enemy of strategic change is ego investment in the way things are right now, meaning that change can threaten a person's sense of satisfaction and even self-esteem. I saw another example of this familiar phenomenon at work just the other day. An ad hoc board committee that had been working for several months to come up with enhancements to the board's governing structure and processes had spent four hours reviewing each of the recommendations with their board colleagues in an intensive work session. There was apparently strong consensus to move ahead. No one questioned the rationale backing up the recommendations, or that they technically made the best of sense.

But as the meeting wound down, the chair of the soon-to-be eliminated finance committee, who was slated to take over the newly created performance oversight committee, noticed that budget preparation was listed in the job description of the new planning committee, whereas it had for years been treated as a finance-committee responsibility. Even though the difference between budget preparation (a planning function by definition) and budget control was then clearly explained—to the satisfaction of all the other board members present—the meeting went on for another hour as this board member asked the same question again and again—ad nauseam. It was clear to me, and probably to everyone else present, that this harping had less to do with the technical merits of the case than with the questioner's ego—specifically, his sense of losing face before his peers.

## BEATING THE ODDS

Experience has taught me that a board can make a powerful contribution to implementing strategic change by playing two related but distinct roles. In the first place, standing back from the fray, wearing their traditional governing hat, board members can provide support to the CEO, who is basically responsible for making sure that strategic change initiatives are carried out. But when the change initiatives relate to the governing function itself—the board's role, structure, or process—the board must play a hands-on leadership role in conjunction with the CEO, who could not possibly carry the ball alone for obvious political reasons.

As backup to the CEO in carrying out the change initiatives in your organization's strategic change portfolio, your board can:

- ensure that financial resources required to implement the initiatives are actually allocated, including backing the CEO in taking such steps as incurring debt, taking money from a lower priority program or service, approaching foundations for funding, and the like. Expecting your CEO to work miracles would fall in the category of irresponsible governance.

- confer legitimacy on the change process, by taking action that provides the change initiatives with official, even legal, status, thereby placing resistance outside the pale in terms of organizational norms. To take a recent example, the board of a professional association adopted a formal resolution authorizing the CEO to "proceed with implementation" of particular initiatives that were described in the resolution as "critical to our long-term competitiveness and in the best interest of our members."

- provide the CEO with visible political backing, which can be extremely critical when controversial recommendations are highly likely to arouse visceral opposition. This kind of support can take various forms. For example, board members can agree among themselves not to engage in any direct dialogue with resisters, always communicating only through the CEO in response to individual questions and complaints. More affirmatively, the board of a large trade association that was engaged in a major restructuring of member dues agreed that executive committee members should publicly back the CEO by appearing with her at four regional membership meetings that had been scheduled to address member questions. These board members were highly visible, but silent, partners whose presence without question buttressed the CEO's standing. "We're 100 percent behind what she's doing in tackling the dues issue" is the message that their presence loudly and clearly conveyed.

## HANDS-ON BOARD INVOLVEMENT

Of course, when strategic change affects the board directly, no CEO in her right mind would lead the change charge, unless, that is, she was driven by a deep professional death wish. Where their own role, structure, and process are concerned, board members only take direction from their peers, and even then, often grudgingly. Many associations and other nonprofits have found that it makes good sense to create a formal program structure to accomplish major changes in governance, lifting the change initiatives out of the day-to-day operational framework and protecting them by creating a kind of organizational carapace. Such program structures are typically ad hoc, in the sense that they are designed to fade away when the initiatives are well on their way to implementation.

For example, I worked with an association board and CEO a few years ago that, following up on an intensive two-day retreat, had decided to implement a major overhaul of its board, including such initiatives as: expanding the board's size by adding three seats for "outside" board members; completely revamping the standing-committee structure, moving from eight silo committees to three broadly functional governing committees; instituting a much-improved process for board evaluation of the CEO; and upgrading the board's role in the strategic-planning process. In light of the scale, complexity, and stakes involved in this change effort, the board adopted a resolution creating the "Governance 20/20 Initiative," consisting of the following key elements:

- **Governance 20/20 Steering Committee**
  Headed by the board chair and consisting of six board members along with the CEO, the 20/20 Steering Committee was responsible for:
    1. reviewing and approving the implementation plan, schedule, and budget
    2. overseeing implementation of the governance initiatives, providing special support as appropriate
    3. monitoring the implementation process and keeping the full board informed of progress and problems
    4. approving major changes in implementation plans on the recommendation of the officer-in-charge

In appointing the steering committee, the board chair didn't fall into the trap of merely tapping the old-guard executive committee. As a conscious strategy to ensure a smoother implementation process, a diverse group of seasoned and "young Turk" board members was assembled, including two of the more vocal critics on the board of the "if it ain't broke don't fix it" ilk. It was assumed—correctly as it turned out—that it would be far better to have strong critics involved in the implementation process than sitting on the sidelines carping.

- **Governance 20/20 Officer-In-Charge**
  The CEO was designated "officer-in-charge" of the 20/20 Initiative, in this capacity basically responsible for providing executive direction to the implementation process and for making sure that whatever staff support was required to keep the process on schedule would be provided. The CEO's appointment to the steering committee also symbolized the partnership between the board and its CEO in the area of association governance.

- **20/20 Program Coordinator**
  Appointed by, and reporting to, the CEO, this member of the senior-management team was responsible for:
  1. developing detailed implementation plans and schedules
  2. providing hands-on support and management of all implementation activities
  3. preparing progress briefings for the CEO and steering committee
  4. recommending action to deal with implementation problems

The CEO wisely chose to appoint a senior member of her executive team to serve as program coordinator, rather than tapping a manager one or more steps farther down the organizational ladder, partly to demonstrate the high priority she accorded to the governance reforms and also to ensure that other members of the executive team would respond with alacrity to the coordinator's requests for implementation assistance. In designating the director of administrative services to play this role, the CEO also made sure that the coordinator was a passionate and experienced project management type with a keen appetite for detail.

## ANYTHING BUT A BUREAUCRATIC MONSTROSITY

When the board originally discussed the Governance 20/20 structure, a couple of members raised the concern that it would just slow the implementation process down by adding a superfluous bureaucratic layer. In practice, the very opposite was true. The dedicated structure ensured that critical decisions received the attention they deserved and were made expeditiously, and that implementation details were meticulously handled, meaning that time wasn't wasted in postmortems and redoing activities that had been botched the first time around.

The Governance 20/20 structure was employed for approximately six months, by which time the new board standing committees were fully functional and could handle the remaining implementation activities themselves.

# CHAPTER 10

# HOW CAN OUR BOARD PARTICIPATE IN A MEANINGFUL WAY IN OPERATIONAL PLANNING AND BUDGET DEVELOPMENT?

## MORE LIMITED PLAYING FIELD

Opportunities abound for creative, proactive board involvement—and the exercise of significant board influence—in the Strategic Change Portfolio process (see Chapter 8). Not so with the more pedestrian process of updating your organization's annual operational plan and budget for the coming year. Moving from the realm of strategic change to nuts-and-bolts operational planning, we find a much more constrained playing field. I don't mean to say that there isn't room for high-level board involvement in the operational planning arena—just that the opportunity to exert influence is far more limited. If this isn't clear to your board—and if board members' expectations aren't realistic—you're very likely to have several dissatisfied, frustrated board members on your hands.

The fact is, the great bulk of the operational planning job has already been done before the annual operational-planning cycle actually commences. As far as I can tell, no nonprofit or public organization in the solar system seriously practices so called "zero-based" budgeting, starting from scratch and throwing all planning assumptions open to serious reconsideration; such an approach would certainly invite a collective nervous breakdown. Operational planning and budgeting—as practiced in real life, if not in theory—is essentially a process of fine-tuning and updating what is already going on: programs and services currently being offered and administrative functions now being performed. Incrementalism is truly the name of the game in annual operational planning.

Despite the obvious limitations of the process in terms of significant board involvement, you've probably heard the annual operational plan and budget described more than once as every board's "preeminent policy statement." This fallacious bit of wisdom might seem at first blush a bit innocuous, but it has caused considerable heartburn over the years, frustrating countless board members and bedeviling many CEOs. In the first place, it conjures up inflated, totally unrealistic expectations that can't possibly be met in practice. Being largely finished at the onset of the planning cycle, and dealing with essentially administrative matters, the operational plan and budget can't possibly be turned into a major expression of in-depth board policy making.

In the second place, your board's paying detailed attention to operational planning and budget detail detracts from higher-level strategic concerns. Over the years, I've seen a number of boards spend more time thumbing through a line-item budget, asking relatively low-level questions, than they spend thinking about their organization's vision for the future and its strategic initiatives to realize the vision. This bit of pathological behavior is probably as much the result of a poorly designed strategic planning process as a lust for line-item detail, but it is certainly encouraged by the "preeminent policy statement" myth.

To be sure, there is important governing work for your board to do in the operational planning and budget development arena even if the process is pretty constrained. Many organizations have cracked the operational planning nut by identifying specific "influence points" where it makes sense for the board to devote time and attention before the full operational plan and budget have been produced. Your board, CEO, and senior managers can agree on these points when developing your association's planning-process design, or what is often called the "plan to plan." If you don't take the trouble to fashion your own design—the schedule of steps in the planning process and the roles and responsibilities involved in carrying them out—then the potential for creative, meaningful board involvement decreases significantly.

## DESIGNING THE PROCESS

The surest path to meaningful board involvement in the operational planning and budget process is detailed design. In my experience, designing your board's role in the process is an excellent job for the board's planning committee, working closely with the CEO and senior executives. Keeping in mind that there is no solid line clearly dividing governing work from administrative work in the planning sphere, you want to focus in the design process on answering one key question: *What governing judgments and decisions does it make sense for board members to make—at what particular "influence points" in the planning process—to shape the content of the operational plan and budget, without impinging on legitimate administrative priorities?*

The key design question is never definitively answered; you can always come up with new ways to fine-tune the planning process, making the board's role more productive and even interesting. This is why, in my experience, many board planning committees hold an annual design session for the purpose of enhancing and refining the board's role in planning, with an eye to taking fully advantage of the board as a resource, as well as ensuring greater board impact. Nonprofit CEOs who are truly board savvy welcome creative board involvement in the design process and are active collaborators, rather than defending their administrative turf against possible board incursions.

## THE INFLUENCE POINTS

In my experience, four influence points have proved most effective in enabling nonprofit boards to play a meaningful role in shaping their operational plans and budgets:

1. updating your organization's vision statement
2. reaching agreement on key revenue and expenditure assumptions
3. identifying major operational issues
4. establishing operational performance targets

An annual 1½- to 2-day retreat (or "strategic work session") that kicks off the planning cycle is a powerful vehicle for involving your board, CEO, and senior executives in generating input for the two parallel planning tracks: the Strategic Change Portfolio process (see Chapter 8); and the annual operational planning and budget preparation process. Two of the most important outcomes of such a session, where operational planning is concerned, are the updated vision statement and revenue-and-expenditure assumptions. A detailed vision of the desired future, in terms of your association's long-term impacts on its environment and its long-term performance targets, sets your managers' sights higher as they update their operational plans, basically by asking them to consider how particular changes in current programs and services can promote the achievement of particular vision elements.

For example, I worked with an association of educational institutions whose updated vision statement included the element: "At least 75 percent of the CEOs of our member institutions will be actively involved in our educational programs." Because the association's board and CEO took visioning very seriously, managers clearly understood that in updating their educational program plan for the upcoming year they needed to deal explicitly with the need to boost CEO involvement, and they did manage to come up with creative enhancements intended to attract stronger CEO participation.

Reaching agreement at the annual strategic work session on the critical assumptions driving revenues and expenditures (e.g., membership and earned-income projections; built-in cost increases, such as planned compensation growth) can serve two major purposes. First, it enables your association to establish financial boundaries within which operational planning will be done. Second, it makes it possible to identify major financial issues that must be addressed as part of the planning process (for example, an estimated deficit that forces consideration of both cost-cutting and revenue-enhancement options).

Many nonprofit organizations have found that it makes sense for the board's planning committee to host a "pre-budget operational planning work session" three or four months after the retreat kicking off the planning cycle, at which board members, the CEO, and senior executives spend a day together focusing on operational-planning issues and performance targets to provide more detailed guidance in developing the detailed financial budget document. I recently observed a highly effective session, during which each of the executives heading departments and major programs made a slide presentation consisting of the unit's mission; a set of performance targets for the coming year; and a description of the major operational issues deserving the board's attention, along with the identification of possible operational responses to the issues. The point of the detailed discussion following each presentation was to provide these senior executives with detailed guidance in moving forward with preparation of their budgets for the coming year.

For example, the vice president of educational programs identified as critical issues in her area a steady decline in attendance at face-to-face meetings over the past five years and a steep decline in the cost of presenting "virtual seminars" involving people at various sites through a sophisticated teleconferencing technology. During the discussion following her presentation, it was agreed that her budget for the coming year should include an array of virtual seminar offerings to supplement traditional educational programming. The vice president of member services also alerted board members to growing national–regional communication problems, which led to a detailed discussion of practical ways to strengthen communication channels.

Many organizations have discovered that by holding this kind of pre-budget operational planning session they can pave the way for effective board review of the finished budget document. Rather than merely thumbing through page after page of financial detail, board members—armed with the information generated at the pre-budget session—can look especially closely at particular parts of the budget document. For example, the plan for implementing the new virtual-seminar program will merit detailed examination, as will the plan for strengthening national–regional communication.

# CHAPTER 11

# IS THERE A VALID ROLE FOR OUR BOARD TO PLAY IN FUNDRAISING?

## INCREASING PRESSURE

The governing mission of an association board in the financial-services industry that I worked with a few years ago stated that among the principal desired outcomes of board leadership were that "our association will be financially stable," that "our revenue mix will become more diversified and less dependent on dues and the annual meeting," and that "our revenues will grow to accommodate changing member needs." Ensuring that your organization is financially secure and capable of meeting its service commitments to your clients or members is a classic board responsibility, and no one would question that paying close attention to your organization's revenues is a valid role that your board should play.

For example, as part of the annual operational-planning and budget-preparation process, your board members—if your board is typical—are most likely involved in setting annual revenue targets by major revenue source. They determine, for example, the proportionate share of membership fees in the total revenue mix and how much net income the next annual meeting and next year's education-and-training programs are expected to contribute to the bottom line. Who would question that this responsibility includes making such decisions as establishing membership-dues levels and setting program fees for the coming year? These are givens in the governing business, just as your performance oversight or monitoring committee, in addition to tracking expenditures, surely watches revenue flows, making sure that the money is flowing in according to the budget and that shortfalls aren't looming on the horizon.

Less clear, however, and the subject of much debate these days, is how involved your organization's board should be in actually generating revenues, beyond the traditional governing role of setting targets and monitoring revenue flows. At the local level, in my experience, it is often taken for granted that board service—especially in fine- and performing-arts organizations such as museums, symphony orchestras, and theaters—includes playing a hands-on role in bringing in the money. This means not only button-holing potential contributors, but also making presentations to foundation program officers and government funding bodies, and even writing personal checks.

Direct involvement in raising money has never been a traditional governing role in the association world, but severe financial pressures and the patently obvious need to diversify revenue bases beyond member dues and earned income from meetings and educational programs have brought the issue to the forefront. This puts us smack-dab in the middle of the never-ending debate in the field of governance between "pure" governing and hands-on doing.

## THE GOVERNING VS. DOING DEBATE

Volunteering is a tremendously important function in the nonprofit world. Not only do we depend on unpaid volunteers to do a wide variety of tasks that otherwise wouldn't get done—at least not as well or as quickly in many cases—but volunteer involvement in organization affairs has also achieved the status of a philosophical tenet. The core values statements of many organizations that I've worked with over the years make the point that active, creative, effective volunteer involvement is an ideal to strive for and resides at the heart of what an organization is all about, above and beyond the concrete contributions that volunteers might make to an organization's operations. Members of organizations of all shapes and sizes in diverse fields volunteer in myriad ways: developing conference programs, reviewing and acting on such technical matters as educational-program accreditation and professional-certification standards, serving as liaisons with key constituency groups, testifying before legislative committees at the state level and on Capitol Hill, just to name a few examples.

You can think of serving on your organization's governing board essentially as volunteering to do a very special and important kind of work: *to govern.* I've defined the work of governing earlier in this book as making decisions and judgments about a small number of truly critical governing "products," thereby answering three fundamental questions—over and over again: (1) Where should our organization be headed over the long run? (2) What is our organization all about right now and in the near future? (3) How well is our organization performing? Governing work flows along major leadership streams: the board–CEO partnership, planning, and performance oversight.

What I call "high-impact" governing boards do this job extremely well, working in close partnership with their CEO and senior executives. Playing a hands-on role in raising money for your organization, although it might be a pressing need and top priority, is absolutely *not* governing work. So we come to one of the most hotly debated questions in the field of nonprofit governance: Should our board be involved in doing non-governing volunteer work, and, if so, what work, and how involved should our board be?

## PUTTING FIRST THINGS FIRST

Practical experience has taught me not to be a purist, and so I have no professional objection to your board's getting involved in doing non-governing work such as fundraising. However, you should be aware that these would be fighting words to scholars, consultants, and practitioners who are all wrapped up in the so-called "policy governance" approach, with its (to me) quite artificial distinction between "ends" and "means." The policy governance camp would have no question at all about hands-on board involvement in raising money being a serious breach of the ends-means firewall, seriously polluting the governing stream and opening the proverbial Pandora's box to who-knows-what meddling in executive matters.

The trouble with hard-and-fast distinctions such as "policy vs. administration" and "ends vs. means" is that they tend to break down in practice because they are so out of touch with the realities of today's world. They establish black-and-white rules that seasoned professionals know must be broken now and then to get the leadership job done, and example after example of sensible, non-lethal line crossings and blurred distinctions prove the case that these ironclad rules were never meant to be slavishly followed. Many highly successful organization boards that I've observed over the years have managed to get truly high-impact governing work accomplished while also involving board members in doing such non-governing work as raising money, by following a few rules:

1. **Make sure that governing is the top priority.**
   Governing comes first to high-impact boards—period. No non-governing work is allowed to dilute or compromise the work of governing, which must be accomplished in a full and timely fashion. In practice, this means that the bulk of board members' time is allocated to governing work—in my experience, 85 to 90 percent. By the way, in the area of raising money, this means your board's paying attention to true governing decisions before any hands-on involvement: for example, setting revenue targets by major source, identifying major new sources, establishing the membership dues level, and laying the professional foundation for fundraising (and for board involvement) by making sure that an appropriate investment is made in the fundraising function (e.g., creating the position of development officer). To jump into raising money without having made pertinent governing decisions such as these would be a gross violation of the first-things-first rule.

2. **Make sure that the non-governing work addresses a high-priority organization need.**
   It's a sad but true fact that many boards have gotten involved in pretty mundane non-governing work, such as actually putting together an annual conference program or physically serving as liaisons with stakeholder bodies by attending their meetings. These gross violations of the governing vs. doing line can't, by any stretch of the imagination, be justified by a priority test. A much stronger case can be made for fundraising involvement, however, in light of both growing financial stress and the resources that board members bring to the fundraising arena.

## 3. Make sure that the non-governing work is truly high-level and a close fit with the board.

Fundraising is a highly complex professional field, involving well-trained professionals in doing such demanding tasks as researching possible funding sources, developing complex legal mechanisms (such as endowment funds), writing grant applications, and the like. The professional fundraising job can't possibly be handled by part-time volunteers serving on your board. What board members can do, very selectively, is:

- help identify potential funding sources, drawing on their far-flung contacts. For example, the board member of a large professional association was personally acquainted with a CEO who was very interested in his company's providing financial support for research that clearly fit the organization's mission, and so she alerted the development officer to the opportunity.

- lobby particular funding sources. More than once I've seen a well-timed telephone call or discussion over breakfast or lunch make the difference in securing a funding commitment for an organization, without remotely violating ethical standards. The typical board member brings a well-developed network to the boardroom, and not to tap this in fundraising would be foolish, to say the least.

- lend stature and influence to presentations. Even if the board officers who generously take the time to participate in a meeting with the program officer of a foundation considering a large grant to your organization are not personally acquainted with anyone at the foundation, their presence can lend weight and credibility to the presentation, perhaps making the critical difference.

## CONSIDER A FOUNDATION

This isn't the place to go into a detailed discussion of the pros and cons of your organization establishing an independent 501(c)(3) foundation with its own governing board to oversee fundraising efforts, but I strongly encourage you to consider this option when evaluating how your organization will tackle the fundraising challenge. The foundation route certainly merits serious attention because it elevates the status of fundraising, which now becomes the preserve of a board created explicitly and solely for that purpose, thereby relieving your governing board of the need to devote hands-on time to fundraising work.

On the debit side of the ledger, however, I've seen more than one foundation board end up challenging the authority of the mother governing board, becoming a serious political and diplomatic problem for the organization. For example, a few years ago I worked with an organization whose foundation board, consisting of high-ranking corporate executives, had begun to question whether the mother governing board had any right to provide specific direction in terms of fundraising priorities. Another foundation board actually claimed the right to determine how the money that had been raised under its aegis should be spent, leading to a protracted and painful confrontation with the mother board.

Of course, a few horror stories need not rule out the foundation option, but they should encourage you to think through the pros and cons thoroughly before moving in that direction.

# CHAPTER 12

# WHAT CAN OUR BOARD DO IN THE AREA OF EXTERNAL RELATIONS?

## A POWERFUL CASE

In my professional opinion, a strong case can be made for involving your board heavily in the external-relations arena, primarily as part of the board's governing role, but also—in a more limited way—in actually doing hands-on external-relations work. In the first place, your organization's long-term success and growth are heavily dependent on building and maintaining effective relationships with an incredible array of key stakeholders. In today's world, image can't easily be distinguished from reality, as you have no doubt learned by now. Your organization is in large measure what its key stakeholders perceive it to be, and even though actual performance will tell the tale over the long run, you can't count on good works to speak for themselves—at least not very clearly in the near-term. This means that image building and relationships with key stakeholders in your environment are a permanent high-stakes matter.

In the second place, your board members are uniquely qualified to play a strong, creative role in building and nurturing important relationships. Skills that helped them make it to the boardroom— most notably communicating effectively and managing diverse relationships—are a rich asset that can be exploited in the external-relations area. And by virtue of their membership on your organization's governing board, they bring a large dollop of authority, influence, and prestige that be put to good use in building and maintaining relationships with key stakeholders.

## THE GOVERNING TURF

Wearing their governing hat, boards that are active in the area of external relations—often with the support of a standing board external-relations committee (see Chapter 13)—can ensure above all else that a detailed statement of their organization's desired image is regularly updated. In light of the rapid pace of change in today's world, it makes sense for the image statement to be updated annually, and an effective vehicle for doing so is the annual board-staff strategic-planning retreat. Many organizations with which I'm familiar employ a breakout group at their annual retreat to brain-storm a detailed image statement by completing the sentence: "We want to be seen as . . . ." For example, one organization leadership group that I worked with recently determined that it wanted the organization to be seen as: "the preeminent spokesperson for the profession nationally;" "highly responsive to member concerns and needs;" "the provider of high-quality services at a reasonable cost;" "innovative in planning and management;" "strongly supportive of effective volunteer participation;" among other factors.

Following up on the retreat, your board's external-relations committee can refine and finalize the image statement, which then provides the basis for setting priorities in the area of external relations and for fashioning detailed strategies to promote the image among key stakeholder groups. In its capacity as your organization's governing body, your board is also responsible for ensuring that adequate resources are allocated to the external-relations function and for monitoring actual performance in this area.

I use the term "stakeholder," by the way, to describe any group or organizational entity with which it makes sense for your organization to build and maintain a formal relationship because of the stakes involved. An association's stakeholder without peer, of course, is the membership, whose satisfaction and continued support are critical to your organization's very survival. Technically speaking, an association's members are the organization, but for purposes of image building and relationship maintenance, it makes the best of sense to treat them as an external entity. Other stakeholders might include sister organizations, regulatory agencies, funders, and legislative bodies.

It obviously makes good sense for your organization to pay the closest attention to building and maintaining relationships with the highest priority stakeholders, and identifying the top-priority stake-holders in any given year is an important governing responsibility for your board's external-relations committee. One organization I am familiar with re-visits the stakeholder list at its annual strategic-planning retreat, at which a breakout group makes a long list of every conceivable stakeholder, and then identifies for each what is at stake in the relationship (e.g., money, political support, collabo-ration, regulatory decisions), the current status of the relationship (e.g., close, positive, productive, adversarial), and initiatives that might be taken to strengthen the relationship. This organization board's external-relations committee uses this rough-and-ready, retreat-generated content in coming up with the top priority stake-holder list for which detailed strategies will be fashioned.

## BEWARE OF WISHFUL THINKING

If wishful thinking is a cardinal sin in the field of leadership and management—it is a particularly dangerous course of action where external relations is concerned. However, over and over again, I've witnessed board members confusing wishful thinking with reality in the external-relations arena. For example, not too long ago, I was sitting with the members of an organization board's external-affairs committee who were flabbergasted by the results of a membership survey that had just been presented to them. Months earlier when the idea of doing a survey had initially been discussed, virtually to a person, committee members questioned the need, saying that their hands-on experience made them confident that the great majority of members were deeply satisfied with the organization's services and that a survey would merely "waste money confirming the obvious."

In reality, not surprisingly, the survey uncovered deep skepticism about the value and quality of many of the organization's services, including its executive-education offerings and the quarterly jour-nal, and indicated that member loyalty to the organization had become dangerously tenuous. I would hazard a guess that this all-too-common tendency for self-deception in the external-relations arena is the result of two factors: a very human desire for good news and the ego involvement of what I think of as "hyperactive volunteers"—the organization's members who devote countless hours working their way up the organization career ladder, eventu-ally achieving that capstone of volunteer effort: board membership.

The only way to guard against this tendency is for your board to avoid making any judgments about your organization's relationships with key stakeholders in the absence of reliable information.

## HANDS-ON NON-GOVERNING WORK

Your board's external-relations committee can guard against board members' becoming overly involved in hands-on external relations work at the expense of governing, primarily by setting very precise targets for hands-on board member activities, making sure that work capitalizes on the board as an external-relations resource while dealing with truly high-priority, external-relations challenges. Organization boards that I am familiar with have effectively involved their members in the following activities without diluting their governing work:

- visibly participating in key organization events to signal the board's commitment For example, many organizations' board members make a point not only of attending major meetings, but serving as presenters and facilitators, thereby setting an example of exemplary volunteer involvement.

- making key presentations when member or client support is a critical issue For example, when an organization board I was working with decided to make major changes in its committee structure and governing functions that were expected to stimulate at least active member interest, if not some opposition, a task force of board members took responsibility to present and explain the recommended changes to members in a series of regional meetings, employing an attractive PowerPoint presentation that had been thoroughly rehearsed.

- playing a leading role in implementing initiatives involving key stakeholders. For example, when an organization in the insurance industry decided to pursue a merger with a sister organization (ultimately consummated), the officers of the board made a commitment to participate in a merger committee involving the officers of both organizations, as the only feasible way to transcend the inevitable resistance of several executive-team members and to keep the merger process on track.

CHAPTER 13

# HOW CAN STANDING COMMITTEES CONTRIBUTE TO HIGH-IMPACT GOVERNING?

## A BIT MUNDANE, BUT VITAL

The topic of board standing committees probably doesn't grab your imagination or send shivers of excitement up and down your spine, but you'd be well advised not to underestimate the powerful contribution that these "governing engines" can make to high-impact governing—or the harm that poorly designed committees can do. Although you will hear debate about whether it makes sense for a board to have standing committees, the question is settled in my mind. I have never seen a truly high-impact board that functioned without well-designed standing committees, and so I have become a passionate committee advocate. I have also, by the way, seen poorly designed committees bedevil board members and CEOs, making it extremely difficult to govern at a high-level and turning boards and CEOs into unwitting victims of bad structural design.

Well-designed standing committees can strengthen your board's governing performance and the board–CEO partnership in four major ways:

1. Committees promote technically sound governing decisions, primarily by enabling board members to get into governing matters at a level of detail that the regular board meeting does not allow. For example, in following up on the annual strategic-planning retreat, your planning committee can pay close

attention to refining the values statement that was brainstormed at the retreat, putting it in final form for recommendation to the full board.

2. Committees build feelings of ownership and accountability among board members through their detailed involvement in addressing governing issues, taking pressure off the CEO to be the only source of action recommendations to the full board.

3. Committees can serve as a very effective vehicle for refining and strengthening the board's governing processes. For example, a few weeks ago I sat in on the meeting of a board's planning committee, at which committee members and the CEO reached agreement on the blow-by-blow agenda of a pre-budget work session involving the board, CEO, and senior managers, at which preliminary revenue and expenditure targets would be reviewed and operational issues would be explored. Not long after that, I observed the deliberations of a board performance-oversight committee, which resulted in a re-formatted quarterly financial report that was much easier for board members to understand and to use.

4. Committees can also help to build a more cohesive board-staff working relationship by facilitating sustained interaction of a less formal nature not possible at regular board meetings. I have also seen committees strengthen the board–CEO partnership by enabling the CEO to develop strong working relationships with committee chairs.

## COMMITTEE DESIGN

The primary job of a board standing committee is to prepare for full board meetings, ensuring that informational briefings and action recommendations are ready for full board review and decision making. Experience has taught me that if a standing committee is to play this important role in a full and timely fashion:

• it must be organized along governing—not programmatic or administrative—lines, corresponding to the flow of governing decisions and "products"; and

• its purview must be organization-wide, cutting across all programs, functions, and organizational units, thereby enabling the board to exercise what I call "horizontal discipline" in its governing work.

Two broadly constituted committees that meet these criteria have proved to be indispensable "governing engines" in my experience: planning (often called planning and development, or planning and program/business development) and performance monitoring (often called performance oversight or management oversight). Your board's planning committee would be responsible for assisting the board in dealing with a wide variety of planning decisions and "products"—everything from updating your association's values and vision statement to adopting the annual operational plan and budget. Your board's performance monitoring committee would be responsible for assisting the board in assessing on an ongoing basis how well your organization is performing financially, programmatically, and administratively. You can easily see that these two committees satisfy the horizontal discipline criterion; each one dealing with the whole organization, not a particular unit or program.

Virtually all boards have an executive committee, consisting of board officers and/or the chairs of the other standing committees. The problem with the traditional executive committee is that it is often treated as a mini-board, which basically screens all information going to the full board, thereby more often than not alienating other board members, who feel less important and out-of-the-loop. Many boards in recent years have turned their executive committee (frequently called the "governance" committee these days) into a committee on board operations, rather than a mini-board, whose primary responsibility is to make sure that the board is functioning smoothly as a governing body. This role is discussed in detail in Chapter 14.

The most effective standing committees that I have observed over the years take very seriously their process-design responsibility, in addition to carrying out their governing work. For example, representing the full board, your planning committee can annually take a close look at the design of the strategic- and operational-planning process of your organization from the board's perspective, identifying practical enhancements that will strengthen the board's participation in making planning decisions. The planning committee might fine-tune the agenda of the annual strategic-planning retreat to make it a more effective forum for the identification of strategic issues. Or the performance monitoring committee might reach agreement with the CEO on enhancements to the program performance reports that will promote stronger board understanding of organizational performance.

## AVOID THE SILOS

Violating the key design principle that standing committees should correspond to the board's governing work, rather than to the programmatic and administrative work of your association, is a surefire way to reduce your board's governing performance. Two types of dysfunctional committees stand out as enemies of high-impact governing: (1) "tip of the administrative iceberg" committees that correspond to narrow administrative functions (e.g., finance, audit, personnel); and (2) "program silo" committees that correspond to major programs or services that your organization provides (e.g., member services, education and training, annual conference, program).

Rather than enabling your board to exercise horizontal discipline in carrying out its governing work, these poorly designed committees narrow your board members' perspectives, chopping their governing work into little pieces that don't add up—not unlike the proverbial blind person who sees an elephant as only an ear, a trunk, or a tail— but missing the whole elephant. This poorly designed structure will inevitably turn your board into a collection of technical advisory committees, in the process actually inviting board meddling in administrative and programmatic detail.

When I encounter a defensive CEO and staff who are wasting precious time defending executive and administrative turf from board interference, more often than not the culprit is a poorly designed committee structure that invites board meddling. I have now and then mused about the reasons why such dysfunctional committees were ever established. The only explanation that I've come up with is that boards were traditionally treated as an afterthought in developing organizational structure. Without seriously thinking through how committees should contribute to governing, boards were allowed to become mere vertical extensions of already developed programs and administrative functions.

## BEWARE OF THE WRONG CURE

Consultants who traipse around the country advising boards and CEOs to avoid standing committees are reacting to the shortcomings of a poorly designed committee structure that promotes meddling or forces board members to spend time figuring out how to keep busy enough to justify particular committees (always the case with a committee like personnel). The only sensible cure, in my professional opinion, for a poorly designed committee structure is a well-designed one that really does facilitate high-impact governing. Taking the extreme course of having your board function as a committee of the whole would mean losing the powerful technical and political benefits that well-designed "governing engines" can produce.

## SOME TRIED-AND-TRUE GUIDELINES

The following guidelines—thoroughly tested in practice—have helped standing committees function at a high level in supporting and facilitating high-impact governing in associations and other nonprofits:

1. Every board member should serve on one, and only one, standing committee—with the exception that during your term as a committee chair you will also serve on the executive or governance committee. If any board members are allowed to avoid committee service, not only will you create a caste system (those who must participate and those who are too important to have to), but also, where smaller boards are concerned, one or more committees might drop below a "critical mass" of members.

2. Only board members should serve on board standing committees. Although non-board volunteers can make a valuable contribution by serving on non-governing committees and task forces, adding them to board standing committees is a sure way to dilute board accountability and erode board credibility. Nothing prevents a standing committee from making use of non-board volunteers by establishing special subcommittees and task forces that report to the board standing committee. For example, one association board planning committee I worked with created a vision-and-values task force consisting

of non-board volunteers who carried out their planning work under the aegis of the planning committee.

3. The standing committees must be the only path to the full board agenda. This ensures that committee work is taken seriously and that committees don't degenerate into mere discussion groups.

4. All reports at full board meetings must be made by committee chairs and other committee members, with the sole exception of the CEO's regular report. This simple requirement not only fosters committee members' ownership of reports and recommendations to the board, but also ensures that committee members do their homework (not wanting, of course, to be embarrassed in public). There is the added benefit of the ego satisfaction that comes from committee members' visible leadership at board meetings.

5. The CEO should assign a senior executive to serve as chief staff to each committee to ensure that the committee is provided with the staff support required to carry out its governing work in a full and timely fashion.

# HOW CAN OUR BOARD MANAGE ITS OWN PERFORMANCE AS A GOVERNING BODY?

## TAKING FORMAL ACCOUNTABILITY

Performance accountability is a hallmark of high-achieving organizations and individuals: They set high standards, monitor their own performance, and take concrete steps to become better at what they do. Boards are no exception. Every truly high-impact board I have ever worked with has played an active, formal role in managing its own performance as a governing body, taking accountability not only for the board's collective performance, but also making sure that individual board members meet well-defined performance targets. Although the CEO must be the moving force behind building board-governing capacity (see Chapter 2), no CEO in his or her right mind would attempt to set board-performance standards or hold board members to account for meeting them. This is a job only your board itself can handle well.

Rigorous board self-management is not only a surefire way to enhance governing performance, it can also help build a more positive internal board culture and a positive public image. For one thing, the members of boards that take accountability for their own performance tend to become stronger owners of their governing work, and hence grow more firmly committed to their governing mission. The internal culture of such accountable boards, in my experience, is also characterized by higher self-esteem and esprit de corps, for the simple reason that the kind of high-achieving people who populate boards are emotionally attracted to setting and meeting standards. After all, that's one of the key reasons for their professional and business success—and for their making it to the board in the first place.

You don't want to underestimate the impact that an accountability culture can have on your board's human-resource development. A question that I'm asked quite often in governance workshops I'm conducting is: "Won't some of the really outstanding people we'd like to get on our board be turned off by the whole idea of being held accountable for their performance? After all, these are pretty important people, and we don't want to alienate them." My answer is always the same: "Don't worry; holding your board to clear, precise performance standards will have the opposite effect. The more illustrious the candidate for board membership, the more attractive performance management will be for him or her."

Boards that formally and systematically hold themselves to account for their governing performance tend to become magnets that attract the attention of qualified candidates. In my experience, the word inevitably gets around pretty widely—among your members or throughout your community—that your board is a cut above the ordinary governing body. Potential board members who highly value their time, and hence are looking for a really productive and satisfying governing experience, will tend to gravitate toward your board because of its reputation for rigorous self-management.

No matter how committed the individuals on your board are to performance accountability, however, formality and structure are critical. Individual board members cannot realistically be expected to hold each other to account, as you well know; life is just too short to take on the task of trying to critique and correct erring colleagues. In the absence of a formally established and managed accountability program, as you have no doubt learned over the years, board members will tend to sit back and tolerate unsatisfactory performance rather than risk alienating colleagues. Your board's accountability program need not be elaborate, consisting very simply of:

1. a responsible committee

2. formally developed and adopted performance targets and standards for the board collectively and for individual board members
3. systematic monitoring
4. continuous improvement

## THE RESPONSIBLE COMMITTEE

Assigning responsibility for board-performance management to a standing committee takes the matter out of the realm of interpersonal politics, making the process of setting standards and monitoring performance politically workable. The boards of many associations and other nonprofit organizations have assigned this responsibility to the board's executive or governance committee (see Chapter 13), in keeping with its role as the committee on board operations. Headed by your board chair and consisting of the standing committee chairs, perhaps other board officers, and the CEO, the executive committee brings both clout and credibility to the performance-management task. You just want to make sure that the accountability-management role is clearly spelled out in the official committee position description, which should be formally adopted by the whole board.

## DEALING WITH COLLECTIVE PERFORMANCE TARGETS

With regard to your board's collective performance as a governing body, many boards that have done an effective job of managing their own governing performance have started with what I call the "governing mission," which as you will recall from Chapter 7 is a detailed statement of the desired outcomes and impacts of your board's governing work, completing the sentence: "As a result of our efforts as a board……….." Board governing mission statements have, for example, included such elements as: "a clear, detailed values and vision statement;" "a portfolio of strategic change initiatives that is updated annually;" "annual evaluation of CEO performance;" "rigorous monitoring of programmatic and financial performance." An intensive board-staff retreat is an ideal venue for developing a rough cut of your board's first governing mission, after which the executive committee can refine it and recommend its adoption by the full board. Thereafter, it makes sense for the executive or governance committee to update the statement every few years, recommending re-adoption by the board.

What the governing mission provides is a high-level checklist of your board's responsibilities. With the mission in hand, your executive or governance committee can go down the list of items, asking: First, are we addressing each element as a board? Second, how well are we addressing each one? Many boards have gone beyond the checklist approach (I strongly recommend doing so) by asking their standing committees to develop more precise board-performance targets for the mission elements within their purview and to bring the targets to the executive or governance committee for review and concurrence.

For example, your board's planning and development committee would reach agreement with your CEO on the strategic- and operational-planning process and calendar, which would define what is meant by a values and vision statement and specify how it is to be updated. Your board's performance oversight committee would naturally be responsible for determining how the annual external audit process will be handled (essentially, how a firm will be selected and how the report will be reviewed and corrective actions handled). Your board's external-relations committee would determine not only how good a job the board had done in updating your organization's desired image, but also whether, indeed, effective action strategies were actually fashioned to promote the image to key stakeholders. And your board's executive or governance committee would be the natural place to handle the CEO evaluation process.

A two-step process for assessing your board's performance as a governing body has worked well in practice: starting with the individual standing committees and then moving to the executive or governance committee for an overall assessment. First, each of the standing committees in a special work session assesses its governing performance in its respective areas, noting problematic performance. Then, each committee develops recommended corrective steps to improve performance. For example, the planning committee of a board I worked with not long ago determined that follow up to the last annual strategic-planning retreat had not been handled well in certain respects, particularly the process of reviewing and winnowing down the list of strategic issues. The committee recommended that the design of the next year's retreat include a more methodical process of brainstorming and analyzing strategic issues and that the planning committee utilize a task force of non-board volunteers to come up with a recommended short list for committee review. The executive or governance committee can discuss the individual committee assessments, develop the final board "report card," and bless the recommended corrective actions that the committees have developed.

## DEALING WITH INDIVIDUAL PERFORMANCE

Many board members, in my experience, feel quite a bit of trepidation about the prospect of evaluating their colleagues' individual performance, worrying that they might offend their peers or, worse, cause someone to leave the board rather than subject himself or herself to performance evaluation. In practice, however, I have never seen individual board-member performance assessment produce negative results. On the contrary, committed, hard-working board members welcome their performance being monitored; after all, formal performance assessment is a way of both elevating the importance of the governing role while also honoring hard work and dedication.

What I have found truly objectionable to those board members who make a real effort to participate productively and creatively in the governing process is a board culture that allows substandard performance to go unnoticed and uncorrected. Not setting individual board-member performance standards and monitoring performance, in the eyes of productive board members, demeans the governing function by saying, in effect, that any level of performance is good enough and shows disrespect for those who do care enough to do their very best in the cause of good governing.

The process need not be elaborate nor in any way punitive to accomplish the intended result of contributing to higher-impact governing work on your board. The first set of individual board-member performance targets and standards can be developed in a retreat, refined by the executive or governance committee, and eventually adopted by the full board. Thereafter, the executive committee can tweak the performance targets now and then. One board I worked with a few years ago included on its list of targets:

- missing no more than one full board or committee meeting during any fiscal year with the exception of a family emergency
- always coming to meetings prepared to participate fully
- participating in the annual summer and winter general membership meetings
- attending the annual two-day strategic work session kicking off the planning cycle
- making at least three presentations per year on behalf of the organization to groups identified by the external-relations committee as key stakeholders

The objective of the monitoring process is to red-flag substandard performance before it becomes habitual and to provide counsel aimed at correcting it, without causing any embarrassment to erring board members. In my experience, it makes sense for the executive or governance committee to make individual board-member performance a formal agenda item at least quarterly, taking a management-by-exception approach. Standing-committee chairs are ideally positioned to observe board-member performance, and one of their key responsibilities should be to bring instances of poor performance to the attention of the executive committee at the quarterly assessment session.

The really good news, in my experience, is that 99.99 percent of board members rise to the occasion. They come to the governing game willing and able to perform the governing role conscientiously, so setting standards and targets is a self-fulfilling activity. The 0.01 percent that falls short is the exception that proves the rule.

# CHAPTER 15

# WHAT CAN WE DO TO MAKE SURE THE BOARD–CEO PARTNERSHIP STAYS STRONG AND HEALTHY?

## A PRECIOUS BUT FRAGILE BOND

Building and maintaining a close, productive, and enduring board–CEO partnership in your nonprofit organization—a true "strategic leadership team," if you will—is a high-stakes matter that deserves considerable time and attention. The health of this most precious partnership easily makes the list of top five factors that determine whether your nonprofit will flourish and grow in today's always changing, challenging world. Of course, all human relationships require conscious, constant management to keep them healthy, but the board–CEO partnership is especially fragile and prone to erode fairly quickly, for two primary reasons.

First, the members of this top-tier team tend to be strong personalities with substantial egos and a propensity toward type-A behavior—not the easiest crew to meld into a cohesive team, to put it mildly. Board members and CEOs can pretty easily rub each other the wrong way, and familiarity has been known to breed contempt, as the old saw says. Second, the issues that boards and CEOs must grapple with are often so complex and so high-stakes that they create a pressure-cooker atmosphere at the top, putting lots of stress and strain on the relationship

In light of what's at stake in maintaining a healthy board–CEO partnership, you would think that careful management of this precious relationship would always be a top priority, but you'd be wrong. Experience has taught me that the board–CEO partnership is more likely to be taken for granted than systematically managed, which accounts for the frequency with which CEOs are sent packing by their boards, at a tremendous cost to their organizations in terms of lost strategic momentum, operational disruptions, damaged public credibility, tarnished reputations, and internal morale problems. In every case of a broken relationship that I'm familiar with, a strong front-end investment in meticulous relationship management would have made the best of sense, but waiting to take remedial action when the board–CEO partnership is already badly frayed is just sticking a finger in the dike.

Of the various factors that determine the health of the board–CEO working relationship, I want to focus on four that have proved especially powerful in my experience: (1) CEO philosophy and attitude; (2) a responsible standing committee; (3) board chair–CEO collaboration; and (4) board evaluation of CEO performance. Other important factors, such as frequent, open, candid board–CEO communication, have already been addressed elsewhere in the literature in adequate detail.

## GETTING THE RIGHT CEO

This isn't the place for a comprehensive discussion of CEO recruitment. The point I want to make is that in addition to the standard attributes and qualifications your board will look for in a new CEO, you want to make sure that the CEO's philosophical and operational views on governing and on the board–CEO partnership are in sync with the board's. To be blunt, if a board hires a CEO who is worried more about defending executive prerogatives from meddling board members than about helping the board realize its potential as a governing body, then building board capacity will become a frustrating battleground rather than a matter of creative board–CEO collaboration.

Making sure that the board and its potential CEO are in sync requires, first, that board members actually understand what they are looking for in this regard (otherwise, synchronization is impossible) and, second, that the matter be explored in-depth during the interview and reference-checking processes. Not addressing this matter during the recruitment and selection process can doom the partnership from the get-go.

To take a real-life example, an association board that I worked with a decade or so ago had found a CEO apparently made in heaven—articulate and polished at the lectern, highly knowledgeable in the association's core business, well-read in the field of leadership and association management, the master of such association management functions as membership development, and more. But during the interview process, no one had taken the trouble to ask probing questions about his views on the governing function and the board–CEO partnership. It didn't seem necessary; after all, he had never run into trouble with a board before, so far as they could tell, and he really seemed to enjoy interacting with board members during the interview process.

Only during this CEO's second year on the job did serious tension develop in the relationship, as a majority of board members grew committed to the board becoming a higher-impact governing body that engaged its members more proactively and creatively in decision making. Confronted with the demand that he provide assistance in helping the board make this critical transition, the CEO showed his true colors. Retreating behind a barrier of formal "we-they" ends-and-means policies (essentially rules), he resisted in every way possible short of outright defiance any deeper board involvement in strategic decision making or the implementation of a stronger standing-committee structure. His idea of partnership, as it turned out, was a clear, black-and-white division of labor between the board's "ends"-focused work and the staff's "means"-focused functions. The break eventually came, but at a high cost that might have been prevented by asking the right questions during the recruitment process.

Experience has taught me that board members' being very direct, listening carefully, and asking follow-up questions to clarify points is the ticket to determining whether there is a close enough philosophical fit to support and sustain a positive working relationship over the long run. For example, here are some important questions that discerning board members have asked their potential CEOs in the area of governance and the board–CEO partnership. Keep in mind that this is only a sampling, and for each question there might be a number of follow-up questions:

- We are really interested in being a high-impact governing board that makes a significant difference in the affairs of our organization. What, in your experience, are the characteristics of a truly effective board? More specifically, would you describe the governing role and governing work of such a board?

- Would you describe how you helped your last board build its capacity to govern more effectively?

- What concrete steps might you take as our CEO to help us become a higher-impact governing body?

- Can you think of any barriers that might get in the way of developing our governing capacity, and how do you think we might deal with them?

- Taking the areas of strategic planning and annual budget preparation, at what particular points—and exactly how— do you think the board should be involved?

- In your experience, what are the characteristics of a really positive and productive board–CEO working relationship?

- What steps can you take as our CEO to make sure that our working relationship remains healthy?

- What are the characteristics of an effective process for board evaluation of CEO performance?

## A RESPONSIBLE COMMITTEE

Assigning accountability to a particular committee for monitoring and maintaining the board–CEO partnership is, as is true in other areas of governance, the best way to make sure that it is taken seriously and doesn't drop through the cracks. In this regard, your board's executive or governance committee is the natural candidate, in light of both of its membership (the board chair, committee chairs, perhaps other board officers, and the CEO) and its responsibility for board operations generally. And the most important item in the committee's portfolio, without a close second, is evaluation of CEO performance (see page 90).

## THE BOARD CHAIR AND CEO

A board-savvy CEO will always pay close attention to his or her partnership with the board chair (or president), not only because of the chair's influence on other board members and formal authority in the realm of board operations, but also because of their shared external relations turf. If the relationship is tense or is dysfunctional in other ways, board members will automatically have questions about the CEO's relationship skills, in my experience, even if the particular chair is a real curmudgeon that nobody gets along with easily. The ability to forge a strong alliance with the board chair is widely considered an indicator of a CEO's interpersonal and diplomatic skills.

For the relationship to have any chance of working, however, the basic ground rules must be clear from the get-go: (1) the board chair (or president) is the "chief executive" of the board and only the board, responsible for leading the board in carrying out its governing mission; (2) the CEO is responsible for all internal operations of the organization, including hiring and directing staff; this responsibility cannot be shared with the board chair; (3) both the board chair and the CEO serve as public representatives of the organization and, hence, must consciously divide the labor in this area; and (4) the CEO takes direction only from the board speaking as a single entity, never from the board chair. With these ground rules in place, it is incumbent on the CEO to take the initiative in building a strong, positive working partnership with the board chair.

The savviest CEOs I have observed over the years always make a real effort to understand what their board chair wants to achieve— the return on the investment of time and energy in chairing the board he or she requires—and then help the chair to realize these individual goals. For example, if the board chair is most concerned about leaving an imprint in the area of strategic innovation aimed at making the organization more competitive, the CEO will make sure that the chair is supported in playing a visible leadership role in the strategic-planning process. In fact, one highly successful CEO I know convinced her board chair to create—and serve as chair of— a strategic-planning-design task force that explored contemporary approaches to leading strategic change. This CEO provided the chair with strong staff support in playing this role, making sure he succeeded. CEOs who want a close, positive partnership with their board chairs will also go out of their way to help the chair succeed in leading board deliberations, spending considerable time with the chair in developing board agendas and making sure the chair is well versed on critical issues.

## EVALUATION OF CEO PERFORMANCE

Regular, formal board evaluation of CEO performance is easily the most powerful tool for keeping the board–CEO partnership healthy, but, ironically, the process is often poorly handled. I have seen board members fill out questionnaires that not only neglect key areas of CEO performance, but also fail to involve board members and the CEO in meaningful dialogue, and—even worse—I have seen board chairs take on the responsibility of evaluating the CEO. The evaluation processes that I have seen work well in terms of relationship maintenance have fit the following profile:

- A standing board committee—usually the executive or governance committee—is accountable for designing and carrying out the evaluation process and takes it seriously, treating evaluation as one of the board's most important responsibilities.

- The evaluation is based on CEO-specific performance targets that have been negotiated with the committee, in addition to the overall organizational performance targets that are established through the annual operational planning process. Not only is it the board's right to have a voice in determining how the CEO will allocate his or her time to achieving particular results (the CEO's value-added), these results are often at the heart of a healthy relationship. CEO-specific targets are typically set in four key areas: (1) public (and perhaps member) relations; (2) support for the board; (3) strategic planning; and (4) internal operations and organizational development.

- The evaluation process includes an intensive committee–CEO dialogue which is principally aimed at reaching agreement on steps that the CEO needs to take to strengthen performance in areas needing attention.

- The committee reports the evaluation to the whole board, with the CEO present, and invites board comment before the evaluation is finalized. Never is the CEO left sitting in an anteroom while board members discuss the evaluation in his or her absence.

# CHAPTER 16

# WHAT ROLE SHOULD SENIOR MANAGERS PLAY IN THE GOVERNING PROCESS?

## A TEAM EFFORT

Whenever you come across a governing board that is functioning at a high level, generating truly high-impact governance, you can be sure that undergirding that board is an executive team actively involved in supporting board performance under the leadership of a board-savvy CEO. Now, I am not talking about merely processing paper for board review. Of course, there is probably not a nonprofit in existence that doesn't involve its executives and the staff who report to them in preparing documentation for regular board business meetings—financial reports, policy recommendations, resolutions, action recommendations, issue analyses, and the like.

There will always be a need for documentation, but if your board members spend the bulk of their time merely thumbing through reams of finished staff work, be prepared to cope with a restive, dissatisfied group of people who are definitely not involved in governing at a high level. Truly effective executive-team support is aimed at helping a board realize its full potential as a governing body, not only doing high-impact governing work, but also finding deep satisfaction in—and feeling strong ownership of—its work.

The executive teams that do an outstanding job of supporting high-impact governing boards, in my experience:

- are thoroughly prepared—philosophically and technically—to work closely with their CEO in supporting high-impact governing work
- interact intensively with board members, primarily through participation in board standing committees
- regularly and formally employ the executive team as a board-planning and coordination committee

## PREPARING THE EXECUTIVE TEAM

CEOs who expect the senior managers making up their executive team to work closely and effectively with them in supporting their governing board obviously can't just issue marching orders and expect them to do the job well. For one thing, executives who are new to the team might have had only minimal contact with the board. And even longer-tenured team members may have acquired only a superficial knowledge of the governing field, and some of them are likely to have become wedded to principles and behaviors that will conflict with the CEO's strategies for building an effective partnership with the board. Unless the CEO makes sure that executive-team members are firmly grounded in his or her governing philosophy and technical approaches relative to working with the board, the executive team is unlikely to function as a strong support arm for the board.

A key step that the CEO can take in this education process is to articulate clearly and in detail to executive team members the fundamental values and principles that guide his or her work with the board and to make clear that executive-team members are expected to adhere to this philosophy. Executive-team members also need a thorough grounding in the mechanics of the governing process, starting with a clear definition of what "governing" means and moving on to the nuts and bolts involved in doing governing work, such as the board's role in strategic planning, budget preparation, performance monitoring and the like; the use of committees as a governing tool; and practical ways to provide board members with a more ego-satisfying governing experience.

As part of this educational process, the CEO can also assemble a comprehensive library of governance materials, making sure that executive-team members are exposed to pertinent publications in the field and even carving out time in executive meetings to discuss developments in this rapidly changing field. The CEO can also make sure that executive-team members participate in pertinent educational programs on various facets of governance, including organizing workshops exclusively for the executive team.

## COMMITTEE INTERACTION

The regular board business meeting provides little opportunity for your organization's executive team to interact with board members, although I strongly recommend that all executive team members attend board meetings as a way of becoming more knowledgeable about the governing process. Committee meetings, however—even if they are held via teleconference rather than face-to-face—lend themselves to more intensive board–executive interaction. In this regard, as I observed earlier, many CEOs with truly high-impact governing boards designate a member of the executive team to serve as chief staff to each of the standing committees. The chief staff to each committee is primarily accountable to the CEO—but also to the committee chair and to his or her colleagues on the executive team—for making sure that the standing committee is provided with the executive support required for it to carry out its governing responsibilities in a full and timely fashion, including:

- providing direct assistance to the committee chair in carrying out his or her leadership role (for example, making a special effort to go through the quarterly financial report line-by-line with the chair of the performance oversight committee before the upcoming committee meeting)
- assisting the committee in developing its annual work plan
- making sure that the documentation required for committee meetings is complete and timely
- ensuring that committee actions are followed up on, including drafting the committee's reports to the board
- developing and reviewing with the CEO and executive team future committee priorities, goals, and agendas before discussing them with the committee chair
- keeping the executive team apprised of committee progress and problems and requesting the support of executive-team

members for particular committee initiatives (for example, assembling conditions and trends information for the planning committee, which is preparing a presentation for the upcoming strategic planning retreat)

## THE EXECUTIVE TEAM COLLECTIVELY

Many CEOs with high-impact governing boards devote an entire meeting of the executive team every month or two (depending on the board's meeting schedule) to board operations. Not only does this make good sense in terms of reviewing upcoming committee and full-board agendas and negotiating the allocation of staff time to meeting committee-support needs, the executive team can also serve a critical quality-control function, reviewing and critiquing presentations before they are made to the standing committees or at special work sessions.

For example, not long ago I sat in on an executive team meeting at which three team members presented their draft of the blow-by-blow agenda of the annual strategic-planning retreat that was to be recommended to the planning committee the following week, including the descriptions of the nine breakout groups that they were proposing be used in the retreat. Not only was the presentation to the planning committee refined and polished as a result of the executive-team discussion, but team members were also kept abreast of a critical governing-board initiative.

Your organization's executive team can also play a productive role in the process of finalizing critical governing "products" that board members have played a role in shaping. For example, the executive team of an international trade association holds a day-long work session two to three weeks after the annual board-staff strategic-planning retreat, at which team members massage and put in better order for eventual review by the board planning committee the rough-cut versions of such governing products as the updated values and vision statement and the list of strategic issues identified at the retreat.

# CHAPTER 17

# HOW CAN WE ENSURE THAT BOARD-STAFF RETREATS ARE SUCCESSFUL EVENTS?

## POPULAR AND POTENTIALLY POWERFUL

Retreats have become a popular vehicle for involving board members, their CEOs, and senior managers in accomplishing high-impact governing work that couldn't be done—at least not as well—in regular board business meetings. For example, I recently attended a 1½-day strategic-planning retreat kicking off an organization's annual planning cycle, at which board members, the CEO, and executive team updated their organization's values and vision statements, reviewed environmental conditions and trends, identified strategic issues, and considered possible initiatives to address them. The return on your organization's investment of time, energy, and money in a retreat can be quite powerful, in terms of not only substantive outcomes such as an updated vision statement, but also process spin-offs such as esprit de corps, satisfaction, ownership of—and commitment to—directions coming out of the retreat, and even emotional bonding among participants.

However, just because you assemble the right cast of characters in an attractive retreat setting away from headquarters for a day or two does not mean that you will automatically realize a powerful return on your investment in the event. Be forewarned: Retreats are high-risk affairs that can easily fall apart, doing far more harm than good, if they are not meticulously designed and conducted. The last thing you need is one of those "retreats from hell" that leaves everyone with a sense of having wasted precious time and energy for naught. I will never forget interviewing members of a client board who had had a terrible retreat experience five years earlier. What amazed me was how long the bad taste had lasted. I heard essentially the same tale from every board member. It went something like this: "We spent a whole morning debating every word in a one-paragraph vision statement and the afternoon pasting green, yellow, and red dots on flip-chart sheets taped on the walls. If you put us through this again, you'll be run out of town on a rail!"

Over the years, experience has taught me that rigorously following five golden rules will ensure that your retreat pays off handsomely for your organization without putting it at risk:

1. Involve key board members in fashioning a detailed retreat design.
2. Employ a professional facilitator.
3. Use well-designed breakout groups to generate content, promote feelings of ownership, and generate active participation.
4. Avoid reaching premature formal consensus or making final decisions.
5. Agree on the follow-through process at the beginning.

## RETREAT DESIGN

Many nonprofit organizations have taken the task of creating an "ad hoc retreat design committee" to ensure board member involvement in fashioning a detailed retreat design: the specific objectives to be achieved (e.g., the identification of strategic issues); the structure of the retreat (e.g., duration; attendance; whether to use breakout groups and, if so, what groups to employ); and the blow-by-blow agenda. Typically headed by the board chair and including the CEO and three to five board members, the ad hoc committee works closely with the retreat facilitator, who, after interviewing committee members and reviewing pertinent documentation (such as last year's retreat report), recommends the key design elements.

The ad hoc committee usually meets only once, either face-to-face or in the case of a national association perhaps via teleconference, to review and approve the facilitator's design recommendations, putting in place a detailed retreat "architecture" that is intended to ensure success and to lower the risk of the event falling apart to virtually zero. In addition to providing input in generating the detailed retreat design, such ad hoc committees have proved to be a useful vehicle for building board-member ownership of the retreat, creating, in effect, an influential group of champions for the event who have had an opportunity to bond with the facilitator.

## PROFESSIONAL FACILITATION

In my experience, a professional facilitator can make three important contributions to the success of your organization's retreat: (1) bringing experience of what works and doesn't work to the design process (e.g., how to structure a vision exercise or particular breakout groups); (2) keeping participants on track, ensuring that the retreat objectives are achieved fully within the time allotted in the design; and (3) assisting in the follow-through process, most importantly producing the follow-up action report. Just imagine 25 headstrong board members and executives spending a whole day or two together discussing highly complex issues on which there are diverse viewpoints, and you can easily see why self-facilitation would be a risky course of action. Professional facilitators are normally seen as objective participants with no particular axes to grind, giving them a leg-up on the CEO or anyone else on the board or executive team who might be tapped to facilitate the retreat. Professional facilitators who are widely recognized as authorities in areas such as strategic planning and governance also tend to command the respect of retreat participants, who are willing to cede authority for the day or days they spend together.

Retaining the right facilitator is one of the most important retreat-design decisions your organization will make, and so I strongly recommend that this be the initial assignment to your ad hoc retreat-design committee. The "retreat from hell" horror stories that I hear all the time are usually the result of choosing the wrong facilitator. In making this critical decision, an organization should review credentials, check references, and even interview candidates for the job. Of course, it would make sense for the CEO to do quite a bit of the legwork, but the ad hoc committee should seriously consider the decision. Understanding the specific methodologies that facilitators employ is a major part of making the right decision. For example, if you will be holding a full-scale strategic-planning retreat that includes updating your organization's values and vision statements, you cannot find the right facilitator without understanding how candidates define values and vision statements and the process they use to generate them. Otherwise, you just might end up with the whole group wasting a morning agonizing over the wording of a paltry paragraph.

## BREAKOUT GROUPS

Well-designed breakout groups can make a powerful contribution to the success of your retreat. For example, I recently participated in a retreat involving nine breakout groups—three meeting concurrently in each of three rounds over the course of 1½ days (e.g., in round one, the three groups were values/vision; conditions/trends; and strengths/weakness assessment). Breaking participants into smaller groups is not only a surefire way to foster active participation and, consequently feelings of ownership, it is also a proven vehicle for generating valuable content. In my experience, the following guidelines will help ensure that the breakout group process is both productive and satisfying:

Assign board members to lead breakout groups, thereby providing them with ego satisfaction and turning them into strong champions in following through on the retreat. To widen board ownership, a different board member should lead each group.

Make sure that the breakout group leaders are well prepared to play their leadership role. You certainly cannot afford to have one or more board members suffer public embarrassment from fumbling the leader's job in front of board and executive-team colleagues. Keep in mind that some of the board members being tapped for the leader's role might never have facilitated a breakout group—or at least the particular ones they will be leading, meaning that they will need orientation and training to ensure their success.

Carefully assign participants to the various groups, not only making sure that each group is as diverse as possible, but also that both interest and expertise are taken into account. For example, if one of your board members has been a prominent advocate of visioning as a strategic tool, you would probably want to make her a member of the vision-breakout group. Along the same lines, it would make good sense to involve your organization's chief financial officer in the breakout group that discusses financial performance.

Require every member of every breakout group to participate in reporting out in plenary session, rather than having the leader or a reporter give the group's report. For one thing, this will help focus participants' minds on the work of their group (knowing they will have to help present the results in plenary session); for another, it will help to make the meeting more interesting and ego-satisfying.

## AVOID PREMATURE FORMAL CONSENSUS

Board members, CEOs, and senior managers naturally tend to like closure and to get pretty uncomfortable when many loose ends are left dangling. So every ad hoc retreat-design group I have worked with over the years has included at least one board member who argues passionately for a retreat design that results in formal consensus on particular products such as a vision statement or a list of strategic issues. I always strongly counsel against giving in to this natural appetite for certainty because of the harm premature formal consensus, much less firm decision making, can cause. Think about it for a minute. You and your colleagues are spending a relatively brief time together grappling with very complex matters that defy easing understanding, and you are very unlikely to have on hand the information you need to make definitive judgments. Does it really make sense, under the circumstances, to demand closure?

Several years ago I participated as a staff member in a retreat that taught me firsthand the dangers of seeking closure in a short period of time. The afternoon of the first day together, breakout groups brainstormed strategic issues in the areas of innovation and growth, current operations, and image/external relations. In the plenary session following the breakouts, participants were confronted with 50 to 60 issues recorded on flip-chart sheets taped to the wall. So far so good: The breakout groups had been amazingly productive and creative in generating rough cuts of really important opportunities and challenges facing the organization. Here is where the retreat veered off course—and ultimately came to grief.

The facilitator informed the group at this point that their job was to come up with the top five issues in each of the three categories, resulting in a list of 15 top priority issues that the organization could tackle subsequent to the retreat. Without getting into the gory details, I will just say that—armed with sticky dots—participants went through an elaborate voting process that did, indeed, result in the identification of the "highest priority" 15 issues. However, the illusion of precision didn't last long after the retreat, as second, third, and fourth thoughts were considered, and within six weeks, the list had bitten the dust. Not only, as it turns out, was precious time wasted in the retreat, but also what could have been an exciting and energizing discussion of issues became a tense voting exercise guaranteed to extinguish whatever good feeling the breakout-group brainstorming had generated.

## FOLLOW-THROUGH

Building a formal follow-through process into your retreat design can ensure that your organization ultimately realizes a powerful return on its investment of time, energy, and money in the retreat. It also saves you from having to reach premature consensus. Take the above example of the retreat that needlessly veered off course because of a poor design that incorporated a forced consensus process. The disaster could easily have been averted by building into the retreat design the following steps that many organizations have taken to avoid the illusion of precision:

- The 50 or so issues that the breakout groups generated, and the points made during the following plenary session discussion, are faithfully recorded in their full, rough form, without any attempt at editing other than to correct obvious mistakes.

- A special issue-analysis task force consisting of executive-team members and several non-board volunteers meets four times over the next three months, coming up with a refined list of strategic issues that is sent to the CEO and executive team, who further refine the list before sending it to the board's planning committee. The planning committee, by the way, has provided the task force with a sophisticated methodology involving detailed cost/benefit analysis that it could employ in developing its recommended list of issues

- The board's planning committee, in a half-day work session, reviews the issues in detail before recommending the list to the full board for adoption, after which the process of fashioning strategic initiatives to address the issues can commence.

So loose ends were tied, decisions were made, action was taken—not prematurely, but through a well-thought-out process.

# About the Author

The author of 14 books on nonprofit leadership in addition to *High-Impact Governing in a Nutshell*, Doug Eadie is founder and president of Doug Eadie & Company, based in Palm Harbor, Florida. His 2001 book, *Extraordinary Board Leadership: The Seven Keys to High-Impact Governance*, received the H.S. Warwick Research Award for 2002 from the Council for the Advancement and Support of Education. Over the past 25 years, Doug has assisted more than 450 nonprofit organizations in building board leadership capacity and strengthening the board–CEO partnership.

Before founding his consulting firm, Doug held a variety of senior executive positions in the nonprofit and public sectors. He also served as a Peace Corps Volunteer for three years, teaching ancient history in Addis Ababa, Ethiopia. Doug is a Phi Beta Kappa graduate of the University of Illinois at Urbana-Champaign, and he received his master of science in management degree from the Weatherhead School of Case Western Reserve University.